From Lemons to Lemonade

David L. Stevenson

TEACH Services, Inc.
P U B L I S H I N G
www.TEACHServices.com ● (800) 367-1844

The author assumes full responsibility for the accuracy and interpretation of the Ellen White quotations cited in this book. Unless otherwise indicated, all scripture quotations are taken from the King James Version of the Bible.

Copyright © 2021 David L. Stevenson

Copyright © 2021 TEACH Services, Inc.

ISBN-13: 978-1-4796-1246-8 (Paperback)

ISBN-13: 978-1-4796-1247-5 (ePub)

Library of Congress Control Number: 2021903157

All Scripture quotations, unless otherwise indicated, are taken from the King James Version® of the Bible. Public domain.

Scripture quotations marked NIV are taken from the New International Version, Copyright © 1973, 1978, 1984, 2011 by Biblica, Inc.® Used by permission. All rights reserved worldwide.

TEACH Services, Inc.

P U B L I S H I N G

www.TEACHServices.com • (800) 367-1844

Table of Contents

Introduction 5

Chapter 1 7

Chapter 2 13

Chapter 3 14

Chapter 4 17

Chapter 5 18

Chapter 6 20

Chapter 7 22

Chapter 8 24

Chapter 9 26

Chapter 10 28

Chapter 11 31

Chapter 12 34

Chapter 13 36

Chapter 14 38

Chapter 15 41

Chapter 16 44

Chapter 17 47

Chapter 18 50

Chapter 19 54

Chapter 20 57

Chapter 21 59

Chapter 22 61

Chapter 23...64

Chapter 24...66

Chapter 25...68

Chapter 26...70

Chapter 27...73

Chapter 28...76

Chapter 29...78

Chapter 30...83

Chapter 31...89

Chapter 32...92

Chapter 33...93

Chapter 34...98

Introduction

My name is David Leonard Stevenson. People call me Dave. They call me David. Sometimes, they just call me to talk.

As I stop and look back at my life, I have been on a journey and didn't even know it!

My favorite book in the Bible is Proverbs. It talks about being wise and making wise decisions. I was doing it all the wrong way until God sat me down and had a long talk with me.

I have always been fascinated with numbers, like seven is complete (Ps. 12:6), three is the Father, the Son and the Holy Ghost (Matt. 28:19), six is Creation (Exod. 20:11), twelve is the disciples or apostles (Matt. 10:1), whatever one prefers to call them.

Proverbs tells us how to make wise decisions. I do understand when people say, "Oh, if I could live my life over again, I would do it different." Like me, I'm telling you, brother or sister, I've been there, and I have the heart scars to prove it. Come with me and allow me to take you on my journey of God's amazing grace and how I have learned to make lemonade from lemons.

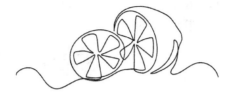

CHAPTER 1

I was born in Nashville, TN, at Riverside Hospital to a lovely lady named Annie Bell Stevenson and my father, Homer Stevenson. I had three sisters and four brothers. Where do I fit in? you ask. I am number seven! I have been intrigued by numbers for a while. I add up things like address numbers, number of kids, how old someone is, etc. Then I see if the total number is of any significance in the Bible. Here is an example using the number 34: $3+4=7$ and 7 is a number God uses to indicate perfection (Ps. 12:6). I always try to see if things add up to a number that is significant in the Bible. You could say it's one of my hobbies. Some people do things different, but for me, I do what gets me past another day.

We were in Nashville for a week, then off to Huntsville, AL, the place I would call home. You can see that I was on the move already! By the time I was old enough to understand things, I was living with three older siblings (my sisters were the oldest and all three had moved out years before) and number eight was on the way. Whoa, wait … I am the baby; this just can't be!

I was beginning to feel, well, you know, a little left out of things. It was not about me (number seven) anymore, it was about number eight. Before I go any further, let me introduce you to my family in birth order. Shirley, Mabel, Ella, Homer Jr., Chris, Clifton, David (that's me!) and Darrell. As I sit and write my story of God's amazing grace, I have lost all my sisters and one brother. There are four boys left and we all live in different states.

My mother Annie was very strict with her children making us say, "Yes, sir" and "Yes, ma'am" and believe me we said it! Today when I say it, some people tell me not to and I kindly let them know that even though Annie Belle is no longer here, she put that mama fear in me, and I will say it as long as I live. Some of you know exactly what I am talking about.

After our school was closed down in Mt. Lebanon, my brothers and I were transferred to school in Hazel Green, AL. We were bused to another town and though I did not really understand what was going on, I was just happy to have a free ride to school and back. By the time I was in high school, I was known as one of the Stevenson boys. My older brothers had paved the way for me. I lived my life as many kids would. I was the class clown and one day it caught up with me.

My mom had told me if I kept acting as a clown at school that she would personally give me a show and a tune to move to. I thought she wouldn't do it since she was getting older. Well, at least that's what I was thinking! As time went on, I remained the class clown until the day Annie Belle showed up! My class had free tickets to the show that would remain in their memories throughout our school years.

My teacher sent me to go stand in the hallway. I was to put my nose in a corner and stand there until … Oh dear, I thought I was standing there until the teacher came back to get me, but as I felt the tap on my shoulder and turned around with a smile, I was face to face with Annie Belle Stevenson! She called me out of that corner and I knew I was in trouble as soon as she said, *"David Leonard Stevenson."* When Mama says your full name, we all know what that means. Immediately I felt the connection! As I turned and saw the look on my mama's face, I knew she was here for business and business only! I couldn't even tell you that day what my mama looked like other than it's show and tell time for real. My mama led me back to my classroom. In the back of my mind I could hear her words to me, "If you want to be a clown, I will give you a show …"

As time went on, I remained the class clown until the day Annie Belle showed up! My class had free tickets to the show that would remain in their memories throughout our school years.

My mama took me back to my fourth-grade class and told me to lay over the teacher's desk. Right there in fourth grade in front of all my peers, Annie Belle had me lay over that desk. There was no getting out of it. No running, no hiding, no pleading. I was helpless and at the mercy of my mama. As I laid over the teacher's desk, and before my first whoopin'(some of you know what I am talking about), Annie Belle looked slowly at the entire fourth-grade class and said, "If any of you laugh or open your mouth about this, you will be next!" This was the day I and my fourth-grade class understood that Annie Belle don't play.

The class didn't laugh that day. As a matter of fact, from the fourth grade when the show started and through my high school years, not one classmate said a word about it. Annie Belle didn't just put the fear in me that day, it seems she put it in the entire fourth-grade class! Some parents are time-outers, some parents are knock-outers and surely you can guess which one my mama was. It had happened to my brother, number five, but I thought that it wouldn't, it couldn't happen again. But it certainly did happen to me that day in fourth grade.

It's strange, but I didn't feel for me that day. I saw the look on my classmates' faces and they looked like they thought they were next! What my mama said to the class, my heart went out to them instead. Well, I can say I did have a different outlook on things after that day. My grades went up. I looked at my mama differently through the rest of my schooling. You could say I learned many things that day!

My mama was a smart woman, raising us five boys who were still at home while our dad was getting sick. Mama would go back and forth to the hospital to visit Dad. She worked as a hairdresser, sold food that she grew in the garden and caught and sold fish to keep food on our table and, my friends, that she did.

Before my dad got sick, he used to bootleg whiskey. Yes, bootleg! To those of you who don't know, this means selling alcohol illegally (in a way that is contrary to or forbidden by law). Yes, that was us!

I remember living in a rental house when I was about seven years old. My dad was having our new home built from the ground up. But while we were waiting on the new house, we moved from the rental house to a shack. Yes, literally a shack. The shack was free, and this helped Dad save money for our new house. It was called a shack and that is what it was. Newspaper was stuck to the walls as insulation. We always had something to read! But that shack gave us many memories.

We had chickens, eggs and a lot of bootlegging going on. Whiskey was hidden under the chicken coop. We also had whiskey barrels hidden in the pond. We sold potato chips, ham sandwiches, pig's feet—matter of fact, pig *everything* from the rooter to the tooter!

I remember one summer we were watching one of those black and white movies on our TV that had the rabbit ears wrapped in aluminum foil for better reception (okay, I know some of you are laughing because you have memories of those rabbit ears as well). Well, that little TV saved us many times while living in our little shack with five boys and two adults—there's that number seven again. Well, our TV would pick up the RPM's on any car, truck or anything with a motor that was coming up our road. The TV would get static and then lose the picture. We learned to count on it. This brings me to the night we got raided by the police.

The chief of police had become a good friend of ours. One reason is because he was one of our biggest buyers of the whiskey. He came to our home one day and said, "Mr. Stevenson, there has been talk around the town about you bootlegging." My dad replied, "Is that good?" The police chief said, "You have to take me seriously. We have orders to come next Tuesday at 1:00 a.m. You have time to get things put up and put in place."

At the time, I didn't know what the rush was about. But I did know, whatever it was, it was happening fast! We were dropping whiskey barrels into the pond, putting some under the chicken coop and cleaning house. And when I say we cleaned house, we *cleaned* house! Now the time had come and we were ready. Two days later they were on their way.

Remember the TV with the rabbit ears and aluminum foil? Well, it was picking up their cars as they moved in closer and closer. So there we were—watching TV at 1 am waiting on the bust. No one could sneak up on us unless they were on foot. The bad thing about that TV was if you were watching a good movie and someone was visiting outside with their motor running, you would have to ask nicely if they could turn their car off.

Boom! As the door was kicked in, the police barked, "Everybody, sit down!" The orders were to search the house. Those were the only orders taken that day! No orders for booze and no asking if they wanted any booze. As they continued to search through the house, nothing was found except disappointment. So, they left the house and drove away.

I had seen God working in our lives many times at our shack on the hill. On one occasion, robbers kicked the door in and yelled, "Get on the bed, all of you!" My brother and I hid under the bed until it was over. You may be thinking, *why didn't the TV pick them up*? Well, it did! On that night, one of my brothers was going out with some friends. The TV was listening and the static started to get quieter, but then just as the TV was going back to normal the static started getting louder again. We were thinking that my brother had forgotten something and was coming back. Nope, that was not it! We were being robbed. These guys had guns and they meant business. Thankfully, no one was hurt. God was certainly with us again. I can clearly see that now. At the time this happened, I knew God existed, but nothing more. Mama took us every week to a Sunday Baptist Church. I would try to get out of going but Annie Belle was not having that. It was more about "doing right" than having a relationship with Jesus. I cannot recall ever praying as a child other than thanking God for our food before we ate. I thought of God as Someone who would zap me if I did not do what He wanted.

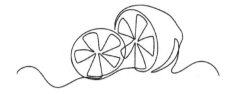

CHAPTER 2

The new house that was being built was almost finished and we were getting anxious to have running water, an indoor bathroom and no more newspaper on the walls. But in spite of all those things, there were moments to remember.

Remember I said I was born in TN and went to AL? Well, we did a lot of that as my dad drove across the state line from AL to TN and back again with whiskey in our car. On one of those trips, during the day, I was hanging my head out the window and I heard my dad yell, "Boy, get your head back in this car!" But before I could—*kaboom*! My head hit a mailbox. Yes, I lived to tell the story and my brain is still working. Thankfully I was too hardheaded and didn't sustain any injuries. As I think of the grace of God, I see He has been all over me.

We had three months to go for the new house! The countdown had begun. At this point, we had started visiting the new house to begin claiming rooms. "This is going to be my room," one would say. "I don't think so," another one would say as he staked his claim. Then Mama would stand and say what she had to say. You want to know what we did when she took her stand? We listened and the only talking back would be, "Yes, ma'am!" God's grace was always upon us all. Three months passed quickly and the new house was finally ready.

CHAPTER 3

As we started to move from the shack to our new house, my dad started to get sick. He had high blood pressure along with many other things. It's like he stayed strong for my mom and us boys until the new house was finished because once it was done, he started to go downhill.

Our new home had three small bedrooms, one bathroom, a living room, a den and seven people living there. You will notice how number seven continues to come up. Dad and Mom didn't sleep together due to Dad's illness. Mom had the den, Dad had one room, two boys had the second bedroom, two other boys had the third bedroom and little brother was small enough to stay in the den with Mom until the oldest brother moved out. He was off to the Air Force.

While alone in the fierce weather we received a call that would change our lives forever. Our father had passed away.

In 1974, I was sixteen years old. April third of that year, Alabama had twelve tornadoes come through the state. One passed close to our home. It was a night I would never forget especially because my dad was in the hospital and my mom was there with him. It was just me and one of my brothers at home. While alone in the fierce weather we received a call that would change our lives forever. Our father had passed away.

I had been preparing myself for that night of loss. While Dad was at home, the doctor would come by and tell my mom that as he got worse, his breath would get shorter and shorter. So, I would go into his room each night and count his breaths to make sure that he was still with us. To this day, I don't like death. I know it's going to happen. As sure as we live, we will die. I guess that's why I choose to be positive. I choose life, in other words. I see the cup half full and not half empty, lemons to lemonade.

Dad's funeral came and went. Now Mom was left to raise four boys by herself. The good thing is she already had us in line for growing up. There isn't too much you could get over on Annie Belle!

I could see our family, as we knew it, was starting to break. Life was beginning to change all of us since Dad passed away and my oldest brother left for the Air Force. It seemed like life was taking us apart.

As I moved on to my high school years, I would ... well, you know when you really didn't like something that your parents got you? I thought I had it figured out. My mom would buy me tennis shoes called Kents. I know many of you remember them. You may have owned a pair also. Well, what all the boys really wanted was a pair of Converse® All Stars, so I would make mine wear out a lot faster than they should have by giving them a little help. When they would tear somewhere, I would help them along by ripping them more.

Well, Annie Belle caught on to me. You want to know what she did? She got me some army boots along with work boots to wear to school. Her words to me were, "Let me see you tear those up." I didn't. Now those boots are still in fashion. You can thank me for that! Yes, those boots were made for walking and I ran in them too.

At the age of seventeen I went to the Lone Star State—Texas for those who do not know—to visit my oldest sister Shirley. While there she introduced me to what the Bible had to say about the seventh-day Sabbath. At first, I was angry with this news because I felt it was an attack on my mother for not raising us in truth. But as my sister continued to turn the pages of the Bible and reveal truth to me, I came to accept it. I also realized my mother had never been shown truth and only kept the tradition of man because that is all she knew. That year I accepted the biblical Sabbath as "thus saith the Lord" and have been a seventh-day Sabbath-keeper ever since.

CHAPTER 4

High school was over, and I was a man. I did my own thing, made my own decisions as I tried to hang on to the words of Proverbs to be wise and not foolish. But it seemed I just could not get rid of being foolish even though I saw God many times coming after me.

God sees the big picture in our life. From God's vantage point, it all makes sense in a perfect way. But from ours, time can seem marked by an endless array of setbacks or move forwardness. In other words, you can look at your cup half empty or half full. We may call it luck, chance or even a random event. Sometimes that is how it seems, but that's not how it is as I have come to understand. Because … are you ready for this? Nothing is random with or to God. He is working out the details of everything even before it happens. He works out all things for our good (Rom. 8:28). God is not just watching it transpire. Check this out. Come closer. I do not want you to miss this. What's more is that God is working out the details towards His intended goal.

I have learned that once I come to the understanding of His overarching goal, I begin to understand to walk in His pathways. In short, God is in control, not me. As we journey on, you will see how I was bringing glory to myself and not God.

It was when I moved from Alabama to Texas that everything went faster. My church attendance also started slipping. Looking back, it just seems that I worked, worked, worked and I did not stick with one line of work. From a concrete truck driver to a self-employed pressure washing business for which I owned a franchise in Dallas and Fort Worth, Texas, and I am just getting started. I was making comfortable money and buying nice things, but there was something still missing in my life.

CHAPTER 5

I continued in my pursuit for meaning in my life. To add to my list of career choices, I became a youth correctional officer with Texas Youth Commission, better known as TYC, a juvenile correctional facility. I took the night shift which was from 10:00 p.m.–6:00 a.m. When everyone else was going home I was just getting my "day" started. That is the way I liked it! No noise and just me and Elmer. Yes, Elmer, my invisible friend who started working with me the day I started at TYC. I know without a doubt that God was watching over me. I still was not walking fully in the commandments of God, but His mercy and grace were on me.

It was on that late-night shift watching over twenty-four young men that Elmer came to assist me. I needed the help and hired Elmer. Well, I guess you could say he worked for free. There was a long hall at my facility. I would put out four chairs after the youth went to bed. One at each end of the hall, two on each side. Because the chairs were not there when they went to bed, the youth really thought that someone was sitting in the chairs. I never corrected their imagination. I had to stay a step ahead of them to keep them from running off on my shift. "Not on my watch," I always said.

Sometimes the youth just didn't know what to think about me or Elmer. One night, one of my co-workers showed up on my night shift. Apparently, he had been out partying and didn't want to drive home. He asked if he could just stay the night and sleep it off. I agreed.

Then it happened.

As my co-worker rested on the sofa, covered in a sheet, you can only imagine how Elmer came to life. About 1:00 a.m. one of the youths came up to the desk. As he was talking to me, the co-worker let out a big yawn. He then proceeded to stretch out his arms, all the while still being covered by the sheet. The youth at my desk asked, "Who is that?" I replied, "It could be Elmer." Let's just say from that point on they believed me about Elmer.

My boss, Travis Wortham, would come in and I would explain why so many chairs were in the hall. He would just laugh. I did, however, get an award for not having any runners on my late-night shift. God's love and God's grace were all over that place.

After spending about three years with Elmer, I was ready to go back into being self-employed. Mistakes, mistakes and more mistakes. In trying to fill a void at home and spiritually, I kept chasing money, certificates and schooling. I was self-absorbed and making things happen—or so I thought. 1 Timothy 1:15 says, "This is a faithful saying, and worthy of all acceptation, that Christ Jesus came into the world to save sinners; of whom I am chief." The New International Version says it this way, "Here is a trustworthy saying that deserves full acceptance: Christ Jesus came into the world to save sinners—of whom I am the worst" (1 Tim. 1:15, NIV). I have thanked God for that promise over and over again. That promise saved me in another way.

I was sitting in my car at a lake during a low time in my life. As I was contemplating driving into the water from the dock, God spoke, "It's not over, David." Not to mention, the thought of water getting in my nose flashed across my thoughts. Any of you who have been swimming and this happened, you know what I am talking about. What a terrible feeling it is! The grace of God reached out to me once again.

CHAPTER 6

The Bible tells us in Proverbs 29:18, "Where there is no vision, the people perish: but he that keepeth the law, happy is he." Sometimes I was given lemons and sometimes I picked my own and there were times that they were just plain thrown at me. No matter how they arrive, it always comes down to what we do with them. I believe many reading this can relate to what I am talking about. Are you going to take the lemons and walk around with puckered lips? Or are you going to make lemonade and make the best of what you have?

> *Sometimes I was given lemons and sometimes I picked my own and there were times that they were just plain thrown at me. No matter how they arrive, it always comes down to what we do with them.*

It's always been my nature to try to be positive in life. If the opportunity doesn't knock, build a door. Some things are lessons, some things are blessings. To my readers: life has many ways of testing a person's will. It can be either by having nothing happen at all or by having it all happen at once. But we should remember the Word of God says in Romans 8:28, NIV, "And we know that in all things God works for the good of those who love him, who have been called according to his purpose." This is for all of us. We just need to take time to stop and listen. My problem was, and still is at times, that I didn't do this. Can anyone relate?

During this time in my life, the 1990s, I met my wife at church. I was blessed with two beautiful girls. It was during this time that I relied heavily on the following self-made phrase, "I don't wait on things to happen, I make things happen." Oh, how I was about to see how wrong I was in saying this! How God can use our words to get our attention. We will come back to reveal how I learned how wrong I was.

CHAPTER 7

In the summer of 1998, I started back up with TYC (Texas Youth Commission) driving seventy miles one way. Keep in mind this wasn't my only job and I was an active father of two. I was there until 2001 and during this time, I was still trying to find myself. Who I was, where I was going?

In keeping myself busy, I signed up with the volunteer fire department. I was busy putting out fires on land as well as in my own household. Staying busy kept the fires at home out or at least more controllable. I just wanted more things to consume my time. I saw many things being on the volunteer fire department. The only thing living I saved was a cat. That counts, doesn't it?

We were in a truck called a tanker. The only thing between us and the inferno was a fence. The fire was coming fast. There was absolutely no way out! The smoke was so thick we just couldn't see.

One time we were fighting the biggest grass fire that I have ever seen. It was burning acres and it was burning fast and hot. Fire needs fuel and oxygen to make it take off. On this day, the fire was burning in a field, heading towards the trees. It was unstoppable so we tried to head it off. Crazy as it sounds, and yes it was, we went right into the smoke as the wind was pushing it our way. We went in and out and around the trees to get in position. It was just the chief and me. And oh, how I prayed.

No one else was around. The fire was getting hotter, the smoke was getting thicker. It sounded like a train coming. We were in a truck called a tanker. The only thing between us and the inferno was a fence. The fire was coming fast. There was absolutely no way out! The smoke was so thick we just couldn't see.

Realizing there was only one thing left we could do, we had to act fast. We decided to empty all the water we had with us along the fence line. *This is it*, I thought to myself. So, we sprayed water all over the fence line where the fire was heading. Now the fire was upon us. The hot, rapidly moving, roaring fire suddenly dropped down and went out. Just as if someone had put out a match with their finger. And on that hot day we were served lemonade. Not because it was given to us, not because we earned it, but because we made a choice to see God's grace and mercy that day.

Are you seeing now how we have a choice between lemons or lemonade? The love of God is greater and goes further than any pen can ever tell. It goes beyond the highest stars and reaches to the lowest parts of hell to pull us out.

CHAPTER 8

After going through the experience of being trapped in a raging fire, it piqued an interest in me to learn about fire behavior. The behavior of fire was to spread more rapidly than ever because of the presence of synthetic materials, which are basically petroleum products in solid form. Fire communicates with us throughout its development, from the beginning of it, until it is done. Remember earlier I mentioned that a fire needs fuel and oxygen to live? I wanted to know more of why they called it "The Beast"!

While working at TYC at night—yes that night shift again from 10:00 p.m.–6:00 a.m.—I was off to fire classes during the day at Collin County Community College. I was interested in becoming a fire investigator.

I thought this would settle something in me; however, I was still not satisfied and kept seeking more knowledge in schooling and different jobs. I was off to Collin County Community College again. This time for building code inspector. I was also taking homeland security classes at the same time. If it was available, able to be used, or obtained, I was on it.

CHAPTER 9

I could not figure out where I was going, but I was sure in a hurry-up mindset to get there. I was working and going to school, going to school and working. Many times, I slept in my car because one of my pet peeves is being late. My days were so full and at times the places I had to go were so spread out that I did not want to chance being late by going home in between. You can tell a lot about a person by how they keep time and what is important to them. Time is of great value and the wise management of it is likely to have a profound effect on success and wellbeing. All the time in my business I was not looking for or at God, but He was looking for me.

I had heard that all things worked together for good. I had heard it over and over again. So why did I feel so unfulfilled? Church attendance was a hit and miss at this point. It was all about me as I tried to fill a void. I was running from God.

Hey! Watch where you're going. That was the problem I had. Deuteronomy 6:5 reads: "And thou shalt love the LORD thy God with all thine heart, and with all thy soul, and with all thy might." I was so far from God and I knew it. I did not want to get close to God because I knew there would be trials and testing. I knew I had not studied God's Word enough to help me go through or overcome these tests. I also knew that I would have to change my current lifestyle and give up things that I liked.

We are often tempted to believe that God has promised to keep us from trials, tests and pain. Then when He doesn't, and bad things start to happen, we feel that God has forgotten us. We start feeling down, discouraged or even defeated. God never ever promised to deliver us from all trials as you will see as you read on.

God did promise that in ALL the things that go on in our lives, we will conquer through Him. He is our protector and our provider. Look at Psalm 23. Look at what David said—not me, the other David:

> The Lord is my shepherd; I shall not want. *[for anything.]*
>
> He maketh me to lie down in green pastures: *[He knows what's best.]*
>
> [H]e leadeth me beside the still waters. *[refreshing to the soul.]*
>
> [H]e leadeth me in the paths of righteousness for His name's sake. *[He gets all the glory.]*
>
> Yea, though I walk through the valley of the shadow of death, I will fear no evil: for thou art with me; thy rod and thy staff they comfort me. *[God has you!]*
>
> Thou preparest a table before me in the presence of mine enemies: *[look at where He's taken you or brought you from.]*
>
> [T]hou anointest my head with oil; my cup runneth over. *[and over again.]*
>
> Surely goodness and mercy shall follow me all the days of my life: and I will dwell in the house of the LORD for ever.

God's mercy is made new for us each day (Lam. 3:22–23). If I'm ever tested, will I pass? Can I pass? We will see … we can't run from ourselves, our problems, or character flaws because wherever we go, they are there. However, I was still running and at high speed!

CHAPTER 10

Not knowing what was ahead of me, while still working with TYC, a job came up with risk management. I would be doing safety inspections for the northern part of Texas. I applied for and got the job. I had my own office; I had a state car I took home and I had my own ego. It was all about what I did! Remember early on when I said I didn't wait for things to happen, I made things happen? I had done all this on my own. Or so I thought.

Even as I write this, I am reminded of so many regrets. But I don't let my past define who I am today. What defines me is the love of God and His plan for me tells me who I am in Christ.

While working with TYC, along with the fire department, I was issued a badge for fire investigator and a police card (which I wasn't aware of) from the chief of police of Quinlan, Texas. Keep this part in mind as life made its continuing journey.

There was a friend of mine that was plotting to kill himself. So I, along with some other friends, thought if we bought his guns, it would give him time to think about what he was saying. We prayed that he would change his mind. He agreed for me to buy his guns and he did change his mind. Remember this also.

One day, on my way to work I got a call from a family who I knew was having trouble with two of their teenage boys. The boys were very big and they were trying to fight with the parents. The parents just did not know what to do. I went over to talk with them and give them some counsel. I decided to bring the boys to my house with my wife and kids for the weekend to give their parents a break.

I had the guns that I had bought from my suicidal friend in my house. Misbehaving kids and guns in the same house are a no-no. Any kids and guns are a no! I never liked them anyway. I had only bought them to help my friend. So, I put them in the trunk of my car. Stay with me. The guns were there Friday before

It was a Texas state trooper and a city policeman who pulled behind me. The first thing they asked me was, "Do you have any weapons in the trunk?"

picking up the boys until Sunday when we took the boys back home. As the sun came up on Sunday, I was getting ready to head to Austin, Texas, for testing on my building code license. But when God has another plan .... There I was driving down the highway with my wife following me in her car. My kids and the boys were with my wife. We were going to stop and eat before I headed on to Austin for my testing Monday morning.

Just as we were getting on the highway, my wife called. Yes, called. We had cell phones then! She called to say that she had a low tire. I pulled to the right shoulder near a restaurant where two policemen were dining. They saw me sitting in my car on the side of the road. I was waiting for my wife to pull behind me so I could check her tire. It was a Texas state trooper and a city policeman who pulled behind me. The first thing they asked me was, "Do you have any weapons in the trunk?" My first thought was, *I don't have any weapons*. And then of course, my answer was yes!

As we talked, the trooper started yelling, "Why do you have these badges? You have more than me! Have you been in the military?" I said, "No." He yelled, "You're lying to me!" I said, "No, sir. One is for fire investigator; one is for correctional officer for TYC." He said, "You're a liar and you're a nobody." *Well okay, tell me how you really feel*, I thought! He never listened to me. He didn't have room to reason because he saw what he wanted to see.

They impounded my car, put me in handcuffs, and put me in the front seat of the Texas state trooper's car. That is when I noticed the camera on the trooper's dash was recording my arrest. He and my wife, who was standing nearby, were holding what seemed like a casual conversation. She appeared calm and unafraid. Her nonchalant demeanor made me feel alone. Why was this happening? It seemed as if I was singled out for no reason. Things just weren't making sense. And I was worried about the children. My oldest daughter was confused. The last thing she knew was that we were heading for ice cream before Daddy had to go out of town for the night. My youngest daughter was really too young to understand what was going on. The teenage boys we were keeping for the weekend were very upset and I was afraid they would go off and lash out, making things even worse.

Then John 16:33 came to my mind about what Jesus said to the disciples, "These things I have spoken unto you, that in me ye might have peace. In the world ye shall have tribulation: but be of good cheer; I have overcome the world."

CHAPTER 11

I was taken to the county jail, shaken, nervous and confused. I thought it was all a joke to shut me up for something. Booked in at about 6:00 p.m. that Sunday, my bail was posted at about 5:00 p.m. the following Monday from a friend who worked with me at TYC. He was preparing to join the FBI. We lost contact, but if he ever comes across this book, I hope he knows how grateful I am for his kind generosity that day.

I was currently out on bail, working and going back and forth to court each month for a whole year. Each month I would hear the same thing, "Mr. Stevenson, we don't know what to do with your case. We will see you next month." It seemed this went on forever. Month after month I would go to the courthouse and come back home again, left with the unknown and trying to live a normal life.

The year of 1999 was going by in a confused state of mind. Y2K made it even more confusing. The year 2000 came and I was still going to court. They couldn't figure out what to charge me with. So finally, the local judge said he didn't know what to do so he was sending it to the Feds. They ended up charging me with interstate commerce after running the serial number of the guns. They said somewhere in the life of the guns they found in my trunk, they came into the state of Texas from another state. Remember, I had purchased them from a suicidal co-worker, then hid them from two bipolar kids. I was helping to protect them and my family. I didn't understand what they were talking about. Did the guns walk in? Did they hitchhike? Who gave them a ride into Texas? The judge clearly didn't care. He sat there rubbing his head the entire time as if we were messing with his golf game.

Then as they were digging to keep things moving forward, I was charged with felon in possession of a firearm. *Stupid is what stupid does*, is all I could think. To cover it all, possession is the state of having, owning or controlling something.

I learned a lot about law that year. I searched and read and searched law over and over again. One question I had was why was I being charged as a felon? Let me backtrack a little here. Back up a little more …. Just a little bit more. I am back at twenty-one years of age. I got into some trouble. There is no excuse for being foolish, but I had one.

I was living with family and, at that time, they could not pay bills or buy enough groceries. There were kids in the house and I knew they needed to eat. Soooo, I was working at a bank and that's where my little trouble came about. I thought that if I borrowed a little money and put it back before they knew it was gone …. I am not going to tell you how I did it, and I encourage people there are other options out there, but it happened right in front of a policeman.

> *You may feel worthless because of your mess ups. But when you meet the God of gods and Lord of lords, the Maker of all, you meet the One and Only. The One who can transform you from the person you think you are, to what He wants you to be.*

Remember I said, stupid is what stupid does? Well, I was putting the money I took, or rather was "borrowing," right back into my checking account with the same bank. I know, I know. That's how they busted me! Caught in the act of doing something that one shouldn't do. They called me to the office, I confessed, and they said for me to go home and someone would be contacting me. They did, I had court and was placed on probation and restitution to pay back the loan that I borrowed. I made it through, paid back the loan and went on my way. Until 1999.

I honestly didn't know I had the title "felon" until the guns in the trunk of my car came up. So, fast-forward to the year 2000 again. One day a letter came in the mail from the Feds—short for the FBI. That letter said it was time to retain a lawyer. Oh, how I needed a BIG GOD. A God of the universe. A God that would not leave me alone. A God that knew my name. A God that knew what I was feeling. God sees us and our mistakes. He also sees what we can become.

You may feel worthless because of your mess ups. But when you meet the God of gods and Lord of lords, the Maker of all, you meet the One and Only. The One who can transform you from the person you think you are, to what He wants you to be. God sees more than anyone else can see—even you. David said in Palm 73:26, "My flesh and my heart faileth: but God is the strength of my heart, and my portion for ever."

CHAPTER 12

I needed help, I needed Scripture, I needed promises. Psalm 20:7–8 reads, "Some trust in chariots, and some in horses: but we will remember the name of the LORD our God. They are brought down and fallen: but we are risen, and stand upright." This verse was especially meaningful to me because nothing in my life was making sense, but I decided to put my trust in the Lord.

The court appointed me a lawyer and more months went by. As time went on, I could see that my case was going nowhere. It was time for some strategy, a plan of action. I contacted at least 100 people to write letters of character reference on my behalf. As the letters came in, I would sit in awe, never realizing how much God had used me.

Here we go! With several character references and the video of my arrest, I just knew people would see through the police officer that arrested me. They would see how crazy it all was by his actions in the video. The officer had stated, "The only way I see things is black or white." Now I know!

Let's get back to that court-appointed lawyer. Well ... I let him go because he wasn't making sense and I certainly didn't feel he had my best interest in mind. Unfortunately, some of you reading this know exactly what I am talking about.

I worked and saved along with borrowing money from my retirement and a friend. Ten thousand dollars was the total for the attorney fees and it came together. God was working, I saw it as things were falling into place. I was able to hire a lawyer for my appeal. Even before the new lawyer came aboard, I was ready for my day in court.

I wanted a jury trial. I just knew they would see through all this. I had faith they would decide in my favor once they knew the facts. So, the picking began. Of course, I wasn't involved in that part. The day was set. My boss from TYC, Travis Wortham, my chief from the volunteer fire department, Ed Ragsdale, and my wife were all there. Elmer didn't show up, at least I didn't see him that day!

When God takes you to something, He will not leave you. God causes all things to work together for good to those who love God, to those who are called according to His purpose (Rom. 8:28). I knew God had many things to do with me, but I ran, ran and ran. I could see God catching up with me. Were any of you ever hardheaded as a kid and ran from your mom or dad? When they finally caught up to you it wasn't ever good, was it? Well, I could leave you here and let you guess what happened, but since you're reading the book, I'll finish the story!

CHAPTER 13

I walked into the federal building that morning, went up to the floor of the court where I was to plead my case (before the world, it seemed). I took my seat with my lawyer and saw the prosecuting attorney with whom I made eye contact. They announced what the case was about and they talked and talked and talked. It went on all day as I just sat there believing it was all a joke and would be over soon.

Remember that I had previously said the camera was rolling in the trooper's car? My lawyer subpoenaed that tape for the jury to watch. I just knew they would see right through it all! The jury watched it one time. They came back and asked to watch it again. I was honestly wondering what was going on in their minds. Why would they need to watch it a second time? It was clear I was innocent and they just needed to call it a day. The joke was over. Right? After all, I don't wait for things to happen, I make things happen! I was quickly learning I could not live by that any longer. I was at the hands of the prosecuting attorney, jury and judge. So, I waited.

> *My faith was about to be tested. I was about to see how much God's love, amazing grace and mercy would reach for me to get my attention.*

My faith was about to be tested. I was about to see how much God's love, amazing grace and mercy would reach for me to get my attention. I had been running from God so long, doing things David's way and I was so far from home. I couldn't make anything happen at this point. It was strange, an unfamiliar place for me. But this is where God had me.

The jury was back, the vote was in. Oh wait, did I mention that the prosecuting attorney in his closing arguments yelled out, "DON'T LET HIM BE ANOTHER O.J. SIMPSON AND GET AWAY"? That's what he said.

Wait a minute! I never played professional football. Prosecutors know what they are doing. Sure, my lawyer objected; however, those words were forever imbedded in the minds of the jury. There was no going back, no erasing what they heard. In their minds, I was another black man getting away with something. The damage was done!

CHAPTER 14

The jury found me guilty as charged. I was to come back in one month for my sentencing. One week, two weeks, three weeks, four weeks went by and back in the court room I stood.

I would be leaving my two daughters whom I always told that Daddy would be around. My two daughters and their mother. I couldn't understand why this was happening. Someone, wake me up, please!

My sentencing was read. Felon in possession of a firearm. Being ignorant of the law is no excuse for not following it. They added the interstate commerce law because the gun had crossed state lines somewhere in its lifetime. They had no idea when. They knew I purchased the gun from a co-worker in Texas, but yet, they were going to punish me for it coming across state lines at some point in the history of the gun. It was all so unfair.

Let me share what commerce is: "the conduct of trade among economic agents. Generally, commerce refers to the exchange of goods, services or something of value, between businesses or entities."[1] "Interstate commerce refers to the purchase, sale or exchange of commodities, transportation of people, money or goods and navigation of waters between different states. Interstate commerce is regulated by the Federal Government as authorized under Article I of the U.S. Constitution."[2] So, don't be ignorant of the law. You can be stopped for anything under federal law that goes across state lines.

When I stood before the judge that day, I knew I was going away for a while. All these thoughts were running through my

1   James Chen, "Commerce," Investopedia, https://1ref.us/1g0 (accessed November 10, 2020).

2   "Interstate Commerce Law and Legal Definition," definitions.uslegal, https://1ref.us/1g1 (accessed November 10, 2020)..

mind in just a moments time. *Who would be there? What would it be like there? No more freedom as I knew it! Who would be there for my girls? How would I explain to them that Daddy was going away? What was my wife going to do?*

The judge sentenced me to thirty-six months. That's 156.429 weeks, 1,095.001 days, 26,280.029 hours, 1,576,801.73 minutes, 94,608,103.7 seconds. It felt like forever! Then I heard the judge say, "Mr. David Stevenson, you have a good work history, involved in your church, haven't been in trouble, a lot of schooling behind you. You have been a model resident; therefore, we are going to let you do a self-surrender." (A self-surrender is when you voluntarily bring yourself to jail or prison to serve a court-ordered sentence.) Hmm, okay! Where do I go from here? I will tell you where I went: the promises of God. Deuteronomy 31:6, "Be strong and of a good courage, fear not, nor be afraid of them: for the LORD thy God, he it is that doth go with thee; he will not fail thee, nor forsake thee." Oh, how I held on to those promises. You know what is so amazing about God? God doesn't lie. God has never lied. God wouldn't lie. God can't lie (Titus 1:2). I built my foundation on that.

When I stood before the judge that day, I knew I was going away for a while. All these thoughts were running through my mind in just a moments time. Who would be there? What would it be like there? No more freedom as I knew it! Who would be there for my girls? How would I explain to them that Daddy was going away? What was my wife going to do?

One thing I did from that point on to help get me through, and that continues to get me through things today, is I looked at God calling my name, David Stevenson, in Scripture. To me, Deuteronomy

31:6 reads as such: "[David (He calls me by name)] Be strong and of a good courage, fear not, nor be afraid of them: [David, don't be afraid of this world or anything else. Don't be terrified of what's happening or because of them.] [For YOUR] LORD [YOUR] GOD, [David, goes with you wherever you go. Never forget this, I will never leave you nor forsake you, David. Do not be afraid of anyone or anything and never be discouraged, David.]" I thanked God for His words. I just had to learn to trust them.

Ships don't sink because of the water around them, they sink because of the water that is allowed to come in. So, now I had to stay afloat on God's words to me. The same words, the same promises that are for you, dear reader. He's never failed me yet. I knew God was calling me to a different kind of journey. I just had to take His hand and go.

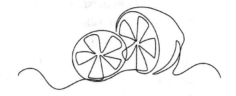

CHAPTER 15

The day came when I was picked up by a church member to be taken off to my new life in prison. While waving goodbye to my daughters and their mother, I cried like a newborn babe and I felt like I needed my mom. However, God had me in a place where I would become solely dependent on Him. David was no longer able to make things happen. David had to wait, wait on God and see how His plan would unfold. When God has another plan, walk on and just say yes.

Pulling up to that large red brick building, the Texas prison, the door seemed so far away. The sidewalk I had to take to check in was so long. Even though part of me kept thinking it was a joke and someone was going to wake me up, I knew there was no turning back on my own once inside. The church member walked down that long sidewalk with me. We arrived at the front desk. I held my paperwork and said, "Mr. David Stevenson for self-surrender." They looked from their computer to me and said, "We don't have you in our computer." I replied, "I knew it was a mistake. I am not supposed to be here." Then after what was the longest ten minutes they said, "We found you." It's good to be found when you are lost, but I knew where I was, and this time it would have been okay to remain lost. However, I would later realize how lost I was and how much I mattered to God. I learned that the Shepherd will seek out that one lost sheep to bring him home.

Accepting the reality of the moment, I waved goodbye to the brother that brought me. It was about to be check-in time. The guard gave me the state "uniform" down to the tighty-whities in exchange for my clothing. *Hey, this is not an even trade*, I thought to myself. I don't wear white underwear and orange jumpsuits …

But I don't think anyone would have listened had I said it out loud. Matter of fact, I don't think anyone really cared.

I took a deep breath as I resigned myself to my new reality. I was ready to run this race whatever way it came out! The guards took me across the yard to show me my room, pillow, blanket and bed. I felt the presence of God there with me as I began this journey I had no control over.

About two hours after I was checked in, a guard came to get me. "David Stevenson, they want you in the front." Does everyone like calling my name? I can't be in trouble, I just got here! They told me that I was being transferred to Fort Worth from where I was in Seagoville. "And why is that?" I asked, "I was put here to be closer to my family." It had been reported that a church member worked there and thus they had to move me. Well, they placed me in a van and transported me to FMC (Federal Medical Center, Fort Worth). From Dallas to Fort Worth was a long ride. So, there I was again, checking myself in. Just as I was getting into the orange jumpsuit, they had me exchange it for khaki pants and a white T-shirt. Okay, I am feeling this. I can do something with these colors. I always said thank you. A thank you goes a long, long way! Now I had my new outfit and they had given me my number which ended in seventy-seven. Just a little nugget that God was with me. Remember when I said back in the beginning that I liked numbers? I especially like the number seven. Seven means completion in the Bible (Ps. 12:6).

I was escorted to a room called THE BUS STOP. This was a room that housed about fifty bunk beds and men to fill them. The men stayed there until they were assigned another room after intake was completed. Of course, no one knew when that would be as it could take weeks. I could see that I wasn't going anywhere fast. So, doing time had really begun. My first day of thirty-six months. How am I going to do this time without losing who I am? Then again, maybe that is what this is all about, losing me and becoming more like Christ. After all, I did have a saying that I didn't wait for things to happen, I made things happen.

Wait just one minute! I have a problem. Psalm 46:10 says, "Be still, and know that I am God: I will be exalted among the heathen,

I will be exalted in the earth." Could God be trying to save me from me? I have always been my worst enemy, always been self-destructive (any behavior that is harmful or potentially harmful towards the person who engages in the behavior). I've learned that God's love never changes, but sometimes His plans for us change our plans.

CHAPTER 16

In prison you must sign up for work detail—at least in the Feds you are required to. A week went by. I figured that doing work detail would help time to move on about its business. So, I signed up for the hospital at forty an hour. Sounds like good money, right? That is, until it's made clear that it's 40 cents per hour! Hey, I didn't complain. If I'm starting to trust God, I have to trust Him all the way, right? Romans 8:28 tells us, "And we know that all things work together for good to them that love God, to them who are the called according to his purpose." I knew somehow, somewhere all of this would work out for my good. I would get paid once a month at $3.25 a day, five days a week, $16 a week, making it $64 a month. God's money came right off the top and was sent out to my church. I had started a savings account before I went into the big house, and it was a good plan.

The big house was a big place that was used for the military at one time. It was then a coed prison and they couldn't understand why or how the ladies kept coming up pregnant. So now it's an all men's federal prison.

Finally, I had my phone account set up to let everyone know how I was doing. About five minutes is all you had on the phone. I would call my kids to talk, but that only lasted for a few weeks and then their mother stopped taking any more phone calls from me, even though I was paying for them. My oldest daughter kept writing for a while until that finally stopped too. Out of sight, out of mind (for whatever reason). I'm sure you have heard that before. Well, let me tell you, it's true. It really hurt to not have contact with my girls. They meant the world to me. But God always sees you right where you are. You are always in His sight.

How did I stay strong during this time? Well, let me share. Strong is what happens when you run out of weak. You will find yourself strongest when you are on your knees.

When it rains, it pours. Y'all have heard that many times. You have probably even said it a time or two yourself! A call came over the intercom, "David Stevenson, come to the administrative office." I was thinking, *what are they calling me for now?* So, I went. I didn't have a choice. NO, I really didn't! When they called, I answered. Why didn't I do that with God before I got here?

I arrived at the big white building to find a deputy standing there with papers in his hands. It was from the courts. Am I going home? No, they were from the divorce court. My kids' mom was divorcing me. I was so hurt as I walked back to my dorm. All eyes were on me. It's like all the men knew what was in my hands.

As I recalled Deuteronomy 31:6, I could hear God saying, "I'm here David. I'm not going anywhere. I'm here until the end." I cried one of those cries where I could have used a windshield wiper to see where I was going. It was a cry that took a lot of Kleenex to blow my nose. Some of you know exactly what I am talking about! People say that kind of crying is good for the soul. It's like a cleansing. Well, if that's true I had a good ole cleansing, believe me. It was just God and me since time waits for no one. I forgave my kids' mom as God has forgiven me over and over again. Again, I found that God was there with me, talking to me.

> *I cried one of those cries where I could have used a windshield wiper to see where I was going.*

Jesus assures us that if we remain in Him, we can be of good courage through any trials or tribulations. He has already overcome the world (John 16:33). I knew God was preparing me for something. I felt like Jonah, three days in the belly of a big fish. I was clearly in time-out. God had tried to get my attention so many times; however, I was too busy making things happen the way I wanted them to. Too busy running! But now I had nowhere to go. It was going to be just God and me for the next three years. I still questioned what brought me to this point. Had I been rebellious or was I out of control? Maybe not physically in my actions, but in my spiritual walk this was clearly a fact.

As the days passed, I continued working in the hospital on the night shift. During one of my many crying nights, God gave me words of encouragement. These are the words that God spoke to me and inspired me to write down as my tears fell to the ground:

> I was feeling down today, got on my knees and started to pray
> Then I started to walk away, I heard a voice inside me say …
> A heavy heart, I've been there
> You called on God, I've been there
> You feel alone, I've been there
> So far from home, I've been there
> Lord, I know You're there for me
> You see the things I can't see
> And I know You're here today
> I hear Your voice inside me say …
> A heavy heart, I've been there
> You called on God, I've been there
> You feel alone, I've been there
> So far from home, I've been there
> God, I know this pain is real
> But I know You love me still
> And I know that You are the way
> I hear Your voice inside me say
> A heavy heart, I've been there
> You called on God, I've been there
> You feel alone, I've been there
> So far from home, I've been there
> Your eyes of tears, I've been there
> Does someone care, I've been there
> Your days of rain, I've been there
> And all your pain, I've been there

"For we have not an high priest which cannot be touched with the feeling of our infirmities; but was in all points tempted like as we are, yet without sin" (Heb. 4:15).

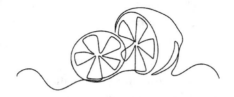

Chapter 17

I've learned to write about my pain and the pain of others and how God works with broken people. We can see so many times in the Word of God how He used broken people and how they rose above their trials or circumstances. God's grace and mercy has turned ashes to beauty many times. That's what gave me hope. God still had a plan for my life! Even though I had dropped the ball so many times in this life game, God kept giving the ball (Scripture) back.

Be joyful in hope. That is what Romans 12:12 says to me. "For whatsoever things were written aforetime were written for our learning, that we through patience and comfort of the scriptures might have hope" (Rom. 15:4).

The knowledge of the Scriptures affects our attitude toward the present and the future. The more we know about what God has done in the years past, the greater the confidence we have about what He will do in the days ahead. And believe me, I was in school learning His ways. Everything was wait. I had to wait on others to shower, wait on others to use the restroom and while waiting you could hear, "How about a courtesy flush?" This would be to show good behavior in one's attitude toward others. I waited in the lunch line, I waited in the commissary line. Waiting became the norm. I was reminded daily that I wasn't in control. I was no longer making things happen.

We had count every four hours, so you better be where you were supposed to! I do have to say, some counts took longer than others because some guards did not do well in counting. But it was just one of those things you let them figure out no matter how bad you wanted to help.

When we do God's work, we bring Him praise. Romans 15:7 says, "Wherefore receive ye one another, as Christ also received us to the glory of God." This text and so many others played a part in my life one way or another—even now.

I had been in prison for one year. I met many friends. One good friend was named Freddie McCrary Jr. I called him MacMac. Nope, I can't tell you what he was in there for. Let's just say he made national news! I still talk to him today. His wife left him as well. You learn to forgive and forgive again. Sometimes people do what they do and sometimes they do what they have to do. There are so many people who are locked up. I could never have made it without my Best Friend Jesus. I know He put Freddie in my life. He supported me a lot while I was in prison. We went many places inside that fence!

Jeremiah 17:7–8 tells us, "Blessed is the man that trusteth in the LORD, and whose hope the LORD is. For he shall be as a tree planted by the waters, and that spreadeth out her roots by the river, and shall not see when heat cometh, but her leaf shall be green; and shall not be careful in the year of drought, neither shall cease from yielding fruit." We can keep going no matter what's happening around or with us if we keep trusting God and taking Him at His Word. We can still be what He wants us to be.

Remember back when I said that God will never leave us? I looked around at nature and … come with me inside the fence. It's okay! Look at all that God has made. There is the dirt on the ground, the grass growing on top of the dirt. There are trees and the same moon that shines on the outside of the fence shines on the inside too. That same sun that shines on the outside of the fence shines on the inside too! The rain, snow, the birds that sing, along with other animals, I saw during my time inside the fence.

Let me share something with you that reminded me God had not forgotten me. One night during my shift at the hospital I was crying. Yes, crying again, trying to understand my mishap and feeling low. Snow was on the ground and there was this rabbit hopping by as I was looking out the window. I said to myself, "Wouldn't it be something if that there rabbit just stopped and looked my way?" Well this little rabbit took a couple of hops and turned right towards where I was standing. He just stopped and looked my way! You can call it what you want to, but I know that God hears us when we call. Things happen when we believe. Remember when Dorothy, from the movie *The Wizard of Oz*, clicked her heels and said, "I want to go home"? They told her that she had the power all the time to go home. Through Christ our righteousness we are more than conquerors. We have the power to believe. The mind has power through Christ. It's where God dwells in us. Look at Philippians 4:6–7 with me to see what it says about our hearts and our minds. The mind is a terrible thing to waste, right? Okay, now to that Scripture I mentioned: "Be careful for nothing; but in every thing by prayer and supplication with thanksgiving let your requests be made known unto God. And the peace of God, which passeth all understanding, shall keep your hearts and minds through Christ Jesus." I was uplifted that night by that little rabbit. I knew God heard and felt my heavy heart on that cold, wintery, snowy night. It's one of those nuggets from God I still talk about to this day!

A lot of times it's the little things we miss. I was luckier than most—I had a roof over my head, running water to drink, and water to wash my clothes and body in. I was able to see the blue sky every day. Some people don't get that in prison, but God is where you are if you allow Him to be. What God was allowing me to see, I would say, is found in Romans 15:17, "I have therefore whereof I may glory through Jesus Christ in those things which pertain to God." Through this God was allowing me to see it was not about me but everything that happened was to glorify God. Jesus is a name to remember.

CHAPTER 18

In Psalm 139 David says this:

> O lord, thou hast searched me, and known me. Thou knowest my downsitting and mine uprising, thou understandest my thought afar off. Thou compassest my path and my lying down, and art acquainted with all my ways .... Thou hast beset me behind and before, and laid thine hand upon me. Whither shall I go from thy spirit? or whither shall I flee from thy presence? If I ascend up into heaven, thou art there: if I make my bed in hell, behold, thou art there. If I take the wings of the morning, and dwell in the uttermost parts of the sea; Even there shall thy hand lead me, and thy right hand shall hold me. For thou hast possessed my reins: thou hast covered me in my mother's womb .... [M]y substance was not hid from thee, when I was made in secret, and curiously wrought in the lowest parts of the earth. Thine eyes did see my substance, yet being unperfect; and in thy book all my members were written, which in continuance were fashioned, when as yet there was none of them. (Ps. 139:1–3, 5, 7–10, 13, 15–16)

God knows us and He knows where we are. Sometimes we don't let people get to know us completely because we are afraid they will discover something about us that they won't like. But our God, the One that created everything, already knows everything about us—even to the number of hairs on our head—and He still accepts and loves us (Luke 12:7). No matter what you have done, you can't erase His love. God is with us through every situation, in every trial, protecting, loving, guiding. He knows and loves you and me completely. I like to say that God is always up to something for my good.

As my days went on behind the fence, I wanted to learn piano. So, I learned! Our thoughts have a lot to do with our future. Here is what I was led to do in order to learn. I took some cardboard and drew all the keys that I could draw on that cardboard: black keys, sharps and flats, white keys, middle C, and A, B, C, D, E, F and G. So, I started playing that cardboard in my mind. The other people would look at me and think, *he's gone, we've lost him.* Then I would go to the library and read how the notes worked. I would then move on to the chapel where there was a piano. Then I would play as I put my fingers where they should go just how I learned on the cardboard that I made. And you know what? I could actually play a song and make music! I could see God continually working on me.

Remember I said that I worked in the hospital? Well, I still did as days, weeks and months went on. No matter how sick you were, you stayed in prison until it was time to go home either on earth or in the earth—in other words, until you were released from prison or you died in there.

One day, or night rather, on my shift at the hospital in my green jumpsuit, we lost one of our patients. An inmate. I had—yes, me—I had to put him into a body bag. I had never liked death since my dad died. I did not understand it, did not care to. But now it was in front of me and I had to face it. With each death a tag was placed on the inmate's toe with his name on it. Every death saddened me with the reality that they were released from prison through death and not going home to their families.

> *No matter who you are or where you are, remember this: when you feel worthless or even begin to hate yourself for what or who you are, God's Spirit is ready and willing to work within and through you. We should have as much respect for ourselves as our Maker has for us.*

I bagged up many after that. I never liked it, nor did I ever get used to it. I needed God's light and was thankful that it helped me while I was in my darkest places. I would think about how much value I was to God and how I didn't want to die there. God's character goes into the creation of every person. You are somebody in God's eyes. I know it makes God sad when someone passes away like that.

Psalm 139:11–12 says, "If I say, Surely the darkness shall cover me; even the night shall be light about me. Yea, the darkness hideth not from thee; but the night shineth as the day: the darkness and the light are both alike to thee."

No matter who you are or where you are, remember this: when you feel worthless or even begin to hate yourself for what or who you are, God's Spirit is ready and willing to work within and through you. We should have as much respect for ourselves as our Maker has for us.

One night as I visited a patient's room to check on him (he had been shot in the back from a drug deal gone bad), he asked me a question, "Mr. Stevenson, I have court in the morning, and I can't sleep. Can you sing me something so I can relax?" I was trying to learn piano; however, there was no piano in the hospital. There happened to be a guitar there though! I had been going to the chapel to play the piano and had tried my hands out on the guitar also. I knew just enough to get by. I had heard if you knew piano, you could play a guitar.

If God can bring you to it … If God can bring you to it, He will bring you through it. I prayed and said, "God, this man has made a request and I need to fulfill it. I must bring it to completion." So, I went to the breakroom and wrote a song just for this patient to help get him through one more day. Just one more! This is the song that was written that night.

We Care

Relax your mind, and close your eyes Jesus is right by your side …
And He will never leave you alone. He will always keep you strong.
Jesus is true, Jesus is real, and He wants to tell you that He feels …
Just look around you, Jesus is here…

And He wants to tell you that we care, oh we care … for you.

Pick up your head, off the floor and leave your worries at the door.

Let me tell you, just what I've found …

Jesus will never, let you down because …

Jesus is true, Jesus is real, and He wants to tell you that He feels.

Just look around you, Jesus is here, and He wants to tell you that we care. We care … For You.

About a week later this patient passed away from respiratory complications. I believe God used me to bring peace to him through music while he was with us. The nurses started letting me go around to visit the sick after this. Some died from cancer, old age, respiratory complications. Some were in wheelchairs. Writing this takes me back there again.

CHAPTER 19

Every chance I got, I would write a song. I loved testing them out at the hospital as they were the ones who really needed uplifting. A few had outside family come to visit; however, most didn't have anyone. The only family they had was us!

One day, one of my friends in prison said to me, "Stevenson, one day before you know it you will be playing the piano for church." Before I knew it, I was playing the piano for church. Never let people tell you what you can't do just because it's never been done, or they think the odds are against you. Hang around people who lift you up, not pull or put you down. By beholding we become changed and that is whatever you behold! But remember this: God is going to have the last word. If we can hope in God, all things are possible.

> *Never let people tell you what you can't do just because it's never been done, or they think the odds are against you. Hang around people who lift you up, not pull or put you down.*

"Therefore did my heart rejoice, and my tongue was glad; moreover also my flesh shall rest in hope: because thou wilt not leave my soul in hell, neither wilt thou suffer thine Holy One to see corruption. Thou hast made known to me the ways of life; thou shalt make me full of joy with thy countenance" (Acts 2:26–28). The point here is that Jesus was resurrected and glorified so we always have hope in Christ! Amen! Amen!

As Matthew 19:26 has said, and still speaks today, Jesus looked at them and said, "With men this is impossible; but with God all things are possible." So, with that in mind, I kept keeping my eyes on God as He was pointing me in the way to go. As I went along my journey there's a song I kept in my heart, even as I write this book, called *The Anchor Hold*s.

We know what an anchor does, right? Oh, you're not sure? It's okay. Let me explain. An anchor is a small piece of equipment in comparison to the boat or ship that it's on. On a ship the anchor is held by a chain, and on a small boat it's held by a rope. The anchor is dropped down into the water to hold the boat steady. Firmly fixed, supported or balanced, not shaking or moving. Does your anchor hold in Christ? For me, those words of encouragement helped to get me through. It kept giving me support, confidence and hope!

As the days went on, I thought all the junk that was going on in my life was a mistake. God did not put me in the mess I made. I put myself there. It came to me that when God was ready to open the doors to go home, He would, and not before. He would also open the next chapter of my life. So, I decided then and there to put my focus on Jesus Christ and not my circumstances.

I started signing up for classes. My first class was a CNA class, Certified Nursing Assistant. Yes, that was me. I had to have thirty-five hours of schooling/training. Next was a typing class along with bicycle and wheelchair repair. Never could I have imagined how God was preparing me for my future. I always loved helping people and learning new things, so I continued to take class after class.

While there in prison I had a few visitors. A few church members helped me along the way. When my mother showed up to visit me, it broke my heart for her to see me there. We both made it through the visit, and it gave me hope. There is nothing like a mother's love. During my time-out I saw my mother one other time. I was so grateful for her love and sacrifice to come all the way from Alabama at her age. I was also grateful to my older sister Shirley as she was the one that left Texas and drove to Alabama and back to bring our mom to see me. I could not put a price on those visits and they just reminded me of God's love for His children.

During this time in prison, I learned to focus on others more and less on myself. God was slowly able to work on my character as I reflected on the person I had become. He was able to chip away at the old man and create in me a new heart. As I pondered this, the tears just flowed and I realized that's how much God loved me. I was so hardheaded, doing what David wanted to do, that God allowed me to be put in time-out so that I could see how much He loved me. "And thou shalt love the LORD thy God with all thine heart, and with all thy soul, and with all thy might. And these words, which I command thee this day, shall be in thine heart" (Deut. 6:5–6).

God gave us Ten Commandments. We must apply all of them, not leaving out one. Come with me to see. Oh yes, I love to rhyme, all the time. Okay, enough of that. Let's look at the Ten Commandments, a divine rule that shows how much God loves us as we stay in check and stay out of trouble in this evil world.

CHAPTER 20

How should man should live? That's you and me. Look how much God loves us. "I am the LORD thy God, which have brought thee out of the land of Egypt, out of the house of bondage" (Exod. 20:2). We all can have this. The following verses give more detail about how God wants us to live. They happen to be the first four commandments:

> Thou shalt have no other gods before me.
>
> Thou shalt not make unto thee any graven image, or any likeness of any thing that is in heaven above, or that is in the earth beneath, or that is in the water under the earth. Thou shalt not bow down thyself to them, nor serve them: for I the LORD thy God am a jealous God, visiting the iniquity of the fathers upon the children unto the third and fourth generation of them that hate me; and shewing mercy unto thousands of them that love me, and keep my commandments.
>
> Thou shalt not take the name of the LORD thy God in vain; for the LORD will not hold him guiltless that taketh his name in vain.
>
> Remember the sabbath day, to keep it holy. Six days shalt thou labour, and do all thy work: but the seventh day is the sabbath of the LORD thy God: in it thou shalt not do any work, thou, nor thy son, nor thy daughter, thy manservant, nor thy maidservant, nor thy cattle, nor thy stranger that is within thy gates. (Exod. 20:3–10)

All these things I knew, and yet I broke every one of them because of my selfishness and yet the Father of fathers called me back home even as I sat in prison. He loved me that much to put me in time-out. I had run and run and run.

> What does this tell me about God?
> What does this tell me about myself?
> Is there a sin thing to avoid?
> Is there a promise to believe?
> How about this: is there a command to obey?

I met people in prison who did not believe. I never try to force anyone to believe in anything. We all have a choice and that's how the love of God works. Love does not force anyone. I can say this: wherever you go, God is there.

One day, we will have to give an answer to Someone.

Do not merely listen to the word, and so deceive yourselves. Do what it says. Anyone who listens to the word but does not do what it says is … [Are you ready for this? He is] like someone who looks at his face in a mirror and, after looking at himself, goes away and immediately forgets what he looks like. But whoever looks intently into the perfect law that gives freedom, and continues in it—not forgetting what they have heard, but doing it—they will be blessed in what they do. (James 1:22–25, NIV)

Amen. Amen.

CHAPTER 21

I was two years into my prison sentence and God blessed me with so many testimonies. I turned them into songs. I love writing and was up to about 1,200 songs. Yes, 1,200 and still writing today. God was opening doors in prison to sing these songs.

"Keep your mind on Me, David," I would hear God say. Romans 12:2 tells us, "And be not conformed to this world: but be ye transformed by the renewing of your mind, that ye may prove what is that good, and acceptable, and perfect, will of God."

I knew that I had about a year to go before I was released, so I needed to get busy. The next thing God gave me was a logo. The HIYH Bird. It is a picture of a heart with the Holy Spirit pouring into it. However, it also reflects the Holy Spirit pouring out. This represents when we allow the Holy Spirit to fill our hearts, we cannot help but pour the love of God out to others. The logo also has prison bars on top. There are people behind physical prison bars and there are people behind prisons they have created or allowed others to create for them. Our logo comes with the statement: There Is Freedom In Christ. HIYH stands for How Is Your Heart. A ministry was started, and the logo was drawn up and sent out for a copyright. Good friends from church, Al Gray and his wife Kari, helped me get it off the ground. I have learned that God knows who you need, what you need and how you need it and He's always right on time.

I had joined the church choir in prison. Most of the time I played the piano, but when I wasn't playing, I was singing. Some of the songs I wrote we sang, some of the songs others wrote we sang, but no matter what, we were singing for the Lord always. We tried to keep our minds on heaven. There were good singers, piano players, base players, guitarists and soloists. Without God we are nothing—nothing! This is as true when I was in prison as it is today.

Jesus said in John 15:1–7:

> I am the true vine, and my Father is the husbandman. Every branch in me that beareth not fruit he taketh away: and every branch that beareth fruit, he purgeth it, that it may bring forth more fruit. Now ye are clean through the word which I have spoken unto you. Abide in me, and I in you. As the branch cannot bear fruit of itself, except it abide in the vine; no more can ye, except ye abide in me. I am the vine, ye are the branches: He that abideth in me, and I in him, the same bringeth forth much fruit: for without me ye can do nothing. If a man abide not in me, he is cast forth as a branch, and is withered; and men gather them, and cast them into the fire, and they are burned. If ye abide in me, and my words abide in you, ye shall ask what ye will, and it shall be done unto you.

> *Things change when you line up with God's will. There may be ups and downs still, but you will know that you can get through it because trouble may come at midnight, but joy comes in the morning (Ps. 30:5). We know that midnight doesn't last long.*

Things change when you line up with God's will. There may be ups and downs still, but you will know that you can get through it because trouble may come at midnight, but joy comes in the morning (Ps. 30:5). We know that midnight doesn't last long.

CHAPTER 22

As I continued to write songs from things that God had shown me, I also found myself writing letters to people on the outside—or should I say, on the other side of the fence. I was trying to keep others encouraged and hopeful. Our circumstances may change a lot; however, God never changes. If I could give someone just a seed of hope and pray that it grows from there, I can rejoice in the Lord because someone's burdens were lifted. Now that's what kept me writing, writing and writing!

As I worked at the hospital and kept going to chapel, my focus was on helping others with their troubles. There is one thing I've noticed, well, two or three actually …. When you focus on others, your troubles don't seem as bad as they once did.

As time went on, my time in prison was getting shorter. I felt somewhat sad because I would be leaving some of my friends behind and some had a much longer stay than others. This made me push harder to write, to sing songs of hope, to uplift, to be a light right where I was.

When something you have been anticipating gets closer, you begin to start counting down the days. It's strange how bittersweet it can be, but you keep moving forward. My three years was almost over. I was looking at the last three months in a halfway house. Why do they call it a halfway house? I am glad you asked! You are halfway between going home and going back to prison. They are supposed to help you get your life in order as you enter back into the "world."

Before I was released, I asked the chaplain if I could put on a concert from the songs that I had written. Not only did I ask to do a concert, I asked if I could do it by candlelight. For those who don't know, they typically do not give a prisoner anything that will start a fire. But the chaplain said yes! So, the week before I was released, I started getting ready. The night came for the concert. I had my songs picked out and videos of Jesus that would go with the songs I had written. Men started coming into the chapel. I stress again, don't let people tell you what you can't do just because it's never been done.

About 100 men filled up the chapel that night. The Holy Spirit was present in that room. The concert lasted an hour. The only light in the room was the glow from the candles. I heard men of all backgrounds crying, some even weeping, and yes, even I was crying as I felt the Holy Spirit moving in hearts that night.

Back to the concert …. It was happening! About 100 men filled up the chapel that night. The Holy Spirit was present in that room. The concert lasted an hour. The only light in the room was the glow from the candles. I heard men of all backgrounds crying, some even weeping, and yes, even I was crying as I felt the Holy Spirit moving in hearts that night.

Some were looking for God, some didn't understand who He was and just how much He loves us and how much He's doing to save us. Then there were some who just didn't seem to care. But it's not our job to try and figure that out. It's our place to love just like Jesus. To show the world, the entire world, what God's character is like.

Once the concert was finished, men came up to me saying they were glad the lights were out. They didn't want anyone to know they had been crying. People, let me tell you, real men cry and it's perfectly alright! When the Holy Spirit touches one's heart, the Spirit of God moves upon that person. It just may be you next! Let God do what God does and that is love. 1 John 4:18

says this, "[P]erfect love casteth out fear." I have been there many times. 1 John 4:16 points out that we should be conscious of God's love. It needs to be more than just a biblical fact for us. We need to experience it each and every day as long as we live.

Sometimes people would tell me, "God must be mad at you for something." Now answer me this. As God is the God of the universe and I am like a grain of sand, why in the universe would God be mad at me when He could just blink, and I'd be gone? Love does not harm, and God is love. Things that happened to me, as I look back, happened to me because of my poor choices. Could we, you and I, have a misunderstanding of God's character? Remember that the devil is a liar and has been since the beginning. So, next time you are going through a hard time remember that God is love and He is not against you. He is always seeking to draw you to Himself.

CHAPTER 23

The day came for me to leave prison. I was over at the hospital saying my goodbyes. Then I heard a voice say, "Stevenson, you got to go, you have to be at the gate by 9:00 a.m." So, I left, saying farewell to all. Arriving at the gate where I came through a few years ago was a very strange thing. The only thing I left with was a few books and the clothes on my back. It was a little strange that I wouldn't be going back to my house with my wife and daughters. Though I knew this for most of my stay in prison, once I walked out those doors it was a new reality—a very hard reality since my girls had been my world.

The day came for me to leave prison. I was over at the hospital saying my goodbyes. Then I heard a voice say, "Stevenson, you got to go, you have to be at the gate by 9:00 a.m."

While I was waiting on my ride, I remembered that Al and Kari said if I didn't have a place to stay, I could stay with them. Another church member, Bob, had said the same. For now, though, I was headed to the halfway house. A new life for me was about to begin. What had I learned during this time? What now, Lord?

Heading to the halfway house I felt I was halfway back into society. It was a different feeling not being locked up but still waiting. I was fine though; I would complete my time here and still grow in the Lord. Three months to spend in the halfway house and time was ticking to get a job, have money, get a phone, get a license and a car. Oh yes, and I had to have something to wear!

During my time in prison I had saved $1,000 for the day I would be going to stay at my friend's place while I got back on my feet. I stretched that $1,000 as far as it would go. God certainly blessed and my needs were covered. I was running because they only give you three months in the halfway house and you had to have everything in order before you left.

I got a job with AAA driving a tow truck. I was grateful for this company in Garland, Texas. They worked with anyone who wanted to work, and I wanted to work! I wanted a job where I could see my girls, take them out, get a place where I could have them over. Well, that only lasted a little while. My two girls were being cut off from me. Child support started the day I got a job and I paid it until the end, but there were always excuses as to why I couldn't see them. During a period of time, they had moved to Oklahoma. I would travel up there when it was my weekend to have them just to be told they couldn't go for whatever reason.

Their mother took me to court to get more child support and during this process I brought up the fact I couldn't see my girls on my scheduled time. My girls got really upset as they were told I was trying to put their mom in jail. It's a hard thing when you are trying to do right and fight for your kids, yet you are getting resistance from them. What do you do? Keep fighting? Don't fight? Either way they aren't going to like you in the end. It was a complicated situation. I just kept it in prayer, seeking God's way and not mine. In the end, that is what matters MOST! There is truly freedom in Christ and when we seek HIS will for our lives, it gives us peace and a freedom that the world doesn't understand.

God had been and was still in control. I was trying to stand up, but something would always knock me back down. But there is something about me and that is the more you tear down my blocks, the more I will try and make them stand the next time—even if I have to glue them together! The wolf—the devil—will always try and blow your house down. With God on our side we can say, "Who's afraid of the big bad wolf?" Nothing can touch you without going through God first. We would do well to remember this crucial fact if we are to grow in Christ. Every day He's getting us ready for heaven by allowing us to see the junk in us so it can be removed. So, let it go, don't hang on to the sin things anymore!

CHAPTER 24

During my stay at the halfway house, there were times I could get a weekend pass for church. That is where I went every time I could. If you look around, you can always see God working in your life if you allow Him to, that's the words of our life … IF we allow Him to!

My first car after coming out of prison was a little Geo. "We all can go in my little Geo," I would say. It was a hatchback and had three cylinders so it didn't use much gas and since I didn't have much money, that was another blessing from God! So, my little go-go Geo, as we would later call it, was a godsend and it allowed me to go where I needed. We were the perfect fit.

I drove for AAA for about a year and was ready to do something different. At this point, I was living with Al and Kari for a few months. That is when Al found out he had cancer. I was grateful they opened their doors to me; however, I felt it was time to go to allow them their space during this time. I also didn't want to overstay my welcome. You know how people can get! Can I tell you what Al was to me? He was love. I had a great respect for Al because there was no guessing with him. If he didn't like you, he didn't like you. If he liked you, he liked you. He was just that way. Al and Kari came to me while I was in prison and asked me if I had a place to go when it was time to go home. I said, "Wellll …." Al said, "I want you to come and live with us." Those words I will never forget even as I write this because Al's cancer took him away from us. Al's favorite song was *The Anchor Holds*. I sang it while he was in the hospital and at his funeral.

When I was still living in the halfway house, I lost another love in the state of Alabama. My mother. It was short notice and I couldn't get a pass in time to leave the state of Texas since I was on probation. Although I will attend a funeral, I don't like them since I lost my dad years ago. That's just how I am. So, the last time I saw my mother, she was alive, visiting me in prison and that's okay with me and my memory of her.

CHAPTER 25

Now it was time for change. I remembered that while in prison I took a class on bicycle and wheelchair repair along with many other classes. I decided I wanted to have a go at it. So, while working at night for AAA, I had time during the day to go looking for something. I came across Loco Motion Wheelchair Repair's shop. I walked in and introduced myself to a man named Tony Wheeler, aka Tony the Tiger. I am always playing with numbers and names so this being Wheeler and wheelchairs, I knew this had to be the place.

I asked Tony for a job and he said he couldn't pay me because he's just a one-man operation. So, I said, "I'll work for free!" He replied, "Let's get started!"

Tony told me the ups and downs as I took the tour to look around. He took me under his wing. I was truck driving at night and learning about wheelchair repairs during the day. I would go on deliveries and learn about that process too. Hours turned into days; days turned into months. I think Tony was feeling bad that he couldn't pay me because he put a little money in my pocket. I told him it was okay because I had known this going in. "Wait on the LORD: be of good courage, and he shall strengthen thine heart: wait, I say, on the LORD" (Ps. 27:14).

Look what Joshua 1:9 says about being strong: "Have not I commanded thee? Be strong and of a good courage; be not afraid, neither be thou dismayed: for the LORD thy God is with thee whithersoever thou goest." Do you believe this? Do I believe this? God doesn't lie, He can't lie. So, what was God up to? I ask this because God is always up to something good for our sake. Tony was a connection for me as I waited.

During that waiting time I signed up for A/C Tech training with the state of Texas. It was a six-month class through Texas Work Force. I started my four-hour-per-day class. I would also continually call a contact that was given to me and I finally was able to reach someone in regard to a wheelchair tech position. I went in for an interview. I told them I was taking a day class for A/C and I would be available to start once my course was finished as I didn't want to waste the state's money. His response, "If you want the job, you have to start now." You know what I told that man? I said, "Okay." I was able to switch my day classes to night classes. Here we go, nights again!

CHAPTER 26

I started the wheelchair tech job working 8:00 a.m.–5:00 p.m. and going to night school from 6–10 p.m. I was learning how to be a tech in both areas. Psalm 100:5 says, "For the LORD is good; his mercy is everlasting; and his truth endureth to all generations." So, I had a choice to make. Which direction do I go? I finished my A/C course but decided to keep working and learning about wheelchair repairs. Plus, it's hot in the Lone Star State of Texas and climbing up into the attics of people's homes … well, it's HOT!

I was a driver with the wheelchair repair company. I was actually able to apply some of the things I learned in A/C class to my work with wheelchairs. My supervisor and mentor was Mr. Joe. Joe taught me to never give up, never surrender to getting repairs done and taking care of the customers. He taught me the rehab side of wheelchairs. He taught me how to modify to improve a product. I listened and learned the business. I wanted to be all I could be for God first and then for the customers that I worked with and yes, for me too! 1 Corinthians 4:2 tells us, "Moreover it is required in stewards, that a man be found faithful." My God was giving me much! You may hear this verse repeated many times in this book, Romans 8:28: "And we know that all things work together for good to them that love God, to them who are the called according to his purpose." The reason is because that's what I hold on to—His promises. I say them, I claim them, I repeat them and I say them again. I guess you can say I wash, rinse and repeat!

I made deliveries. I did repairs. God works and prepares the way before we go. God was teaching me and showing me things in life. I was finally ready to listen since my stay in prison. I owed so much to God as I kept on moving forward on my journey. I kept writing songs and yes, there were mistakes I continued to make. For you and me, and if there's a we, I want you to listen. Most of the time we don't know what we need. We feel we do; we know our wants and our wants and needs get mingled together and can end up in a disaster. Someone gets hurts. That can happen from not waiting on God or hearing from God. Look at Proverbs 4:1, "Hear, ye children, the instruction of a father, and attend to know understanding." Again, I didn't listen, I thought I knew. I got into a relationship that I knew wasn't God's way. I thought I could fix it and go beyond the God of the universe. After all, I was me and He was He. Well, disaster happened and someone got hurt in the relationship. If we stay in God's Word, He guides us in all things, in all truths. Come with me as we look at Titus 3:4–8:

> But after that the kindness and love of God our Saviour toward man appeared, not by works of righteousness which we have done, but according to his mercy he saved us, by the washing of regeneration, and renewing of the Holy Ghost; which he shed on us abundantly through Jesus Christ our Saviour; that being justified by his grace, we should be made heirs according to the hope of eternal life. This is a faithful saying, and these things I will that thou affirm constantly, that they which have believed in God might be careful to maintain good works. These things are good and profitable unto men.

"This is a trustworthy saying. I want to stress these things so that those who have trusted in God may be careful to devote themselves to doing what is good. These things are excellent and profitable for everyone" (Titus 3:8, NIV). Brother and sisters, that's talking about you and me! We can do nothing of ourselves. We mess things up without God guiding us to the door and out the door. He's the truth, the light, the way and the door. You may see something different, but it sounds clear to me that there is not another way. Jesus pleads with us, "Let me have this." The Lord spoke from Genesis to Revelation, "Listen, listen, listen to Me." But as children, we want it our way. Hey, don't they say that at Burger King? Look what Jesus says about listening and hearing His words and applying them. Jesus spoke, "And if any man hear my words, and believe not, I judge him not: for I came not to judge the world, but to save the world. He that rejecteth me, and receiveth not my words, hath one that judgeth him: the word that I have spoken, the same shall judge him in the last day" (John 12:47–48). We have to decide now which side we want to be on! Here is the 911 of the life we live. The consequences of our decision will be chosen by us. I have had many blessings and learned many lessons. A lesson is a structured period of time where learning is intended to occur. It involves one or more students being taught by a teacher or instructor. The question is, who's your teacher or instructor?

CHAPTER 27

In and out of relationships is not healthy. As I kept on writing songs about life and how God had pulled me through my "foolish is, foolish does" actions and my own choices, I kept pushing forward as a tech and as a student of the Lord. As a wheelchair tech I met a lot of people who were either sick or dying. I had a shocking call to come pick up a bed, a hospital bed. When we arrived to pick it up, the body was still on the bed and they wanted me to move it. Well, what do you think I did? You are right, for those who thought I left the body! Yes, I did, and I called back to the office to notify them. I was advised to inform the family that they had to move the body.

I have seen many things in this business, but I have found my calling in serving others. I worked five days a week and had weekends off unless I was on call. Being on call mainly consisted of taking out O2 to help keep someone alive. It was such a blessing to know that I was helping someone.

Once every five weeks was my time to be on call. Some Sabbaths I had to leave right after church in the work van. Dave the Rave to the rescue! I wasn't about to lose anyone on my watch. Time went on and on went time. I got my own place which was another blessing because of how God worked things out. My boss had rental places and I would work on them after hours. He worked out a deal for me on one of his condos. I didn't have furniture or anything for a house really, but that was fine with me. I was finally blessed with my own place. I found a mattress that someone tossed out, a table, a dryer, washer and a bed. God was moving still again and again! It's so true that one man's, well maybe two or three men's junk is another man's treasure. As God gave it, I gratefully took it and used it!

My own home. Remember now, when I left prison, I had nothing, but I knew God would restore in my seeking Him. Wait, David, and keep being faithful. I was all I needed to be with God. I did not, and still do not, deserve anything for the way I have treated God. The GREAT I AM! Who am I, what am I, that He still calls me by name? If the Lord loves me this much then He must love me a lot. He says in Ephesians 5:2, "And walk in love, as Christ also hath loved us, and hath given himself for us an offering and a sacrifice to God for a sweetsmelling savour."

Jesus' love went beyond affection to self-sacrificing service. He loved us so much that His blood was shed for me, you, the world. I saw something in a lady's eyes when I was talking about her baby lambs that she had to bottle feed. It broke her heart to think how she would feel to kill that lamb. That is how sin should make us feel. You may say, "Well ...." A well goes deep. The love of God goes even deeper!

To make it short for you, I worked four years for the wheelchair repair company. They knew that I kept the seventh-day Sabbath as the Lord commanded. One day my boss came to me and said, "David, they are going to start working on your Sabbath." "Well, I don't have a Sabbath," I said, "It's God's day that He asked me to keep." In love I shared that God doesn't force us, so how could he or anyone with the company force me? They pushed for me to work on God's Sabbath, but I would not budge. I offered to work on Sunday if need be. Job 17:9 says, "The righteous also shall hold on his way, and he that hath clean hands shall be stronger and stronger." So again, I did some more growing along my journey. It was then that I started my own business, HIYH Medical Services & Repairs, LLC. My wife kept telling me, "If you are going to walk on water you must get out of the boat." Well, sometimes God helps us out of the boat. That day, I walked in faith and God has been leading us ever since. More on this in chapter 29!

Prior to prison and during my time in prison, as I waited to see what the court was going to do with me, brother Bob Lewis and his wife Sheryl had been praying for me and my family. They had asked their daughter Tiffany to pray for me as well. 1 Peter 3:12 says this, "For the eyes of the Lord are over the righteous, and his ears are open unto their prayers: but the face of the Lord is against them that do evil." Well, as my journey in life continued, that beautiful lady named Tiffany eventually became my bride. She had been praying for me and we didn't even know each other. She had no idea what God had planned for her. She had no idea that her future included me!

Tiffany had three daughters and I had two daughters and when we all got together, we became the Stevenson bunch! At this time, my relationship with my daughters had somewhat evened out. My oldest daughter even lived with us at one point. The only males in the family were me and a dog named Snickers. Snickers did not let just anyone near "his girls," but he allowed me in! It is so good to have a praying family and to know that you are loved.

CHAPTER 28

The time had come to move on from that little condo God had so graciously provided. We all stayed there while we waited patiently to close on our new family home! God's timing was perfect as we had been looking and looking at homes that would fit our needs and even our hearts' desires. We came across one that fit us well. It was all we needed and even had our hearts' desires too. The funny thing is that the house was everything my wife had told our current realtor we needed and wanted and in the price range too. She thought my wife was asking for a lot for nothing, but little did she know the God we served. We never got discouraged and walked in faith knowing God was up to something and He was going to deliver.

When we first saw the home, it was empty and we walked around, looking at it. It had been empty for several years at this point. My wife called a friend of hers that had just become a realtor and asked her to find out the details and see if we could look at it. The day came and we met the realtor, walked in, out and around the house. My wife and I both liked it and believed this was the house God had for us.

One of the secrets to change is to not focus all of your energy on fighting the old, but on building the new. Brothers and sisters, I have some building to do! So, I walked around the house seven times. Seven is complete in the Word of God and He's the same God now as He was back then. I was claiming this home to be ours. Days passed with nights as we waited to see if they would accept our offer. The current owner was in the military out of the country and it was a short sale. Short sales can be quick or they can take a long time. Either way, it was in God's hands and we knew HIS perfect timing is what we wanted.

As we waited, I decided to go plant a baby tree on the property. I also did some cleaning around the house. I learned that there were three gifts that I could control that day whether we got the house or not. I could control my thoughts, my speech and my behavior. Then we got the call. The deal had been completed. The house was ours! It all worked out for our good. Days were slowly passing by as I was giving up who I was to who I could become in Christ.

Chapter 29

With the help of my wife Tiffany can I, may I, talk a little about faith? Hebrews 11:1 tells us, "Now faith is the substance of things hoped for, the evidence of things not seen." You got to have someone that you know can deliver. Who is your hope in? Look what Mark 11:22–24 says:

> And Jesus answering saith unto them, Have faith in God. For verily I say unto you, That whosoever shall say unto this mountain, Be thou removed, and be thou cast into the sea; and shall not doubt in his heart, but shall believe that those things which he saith shall come to pass; he shall have whatsoever he saith. Therefore I say unto you, What things soever ye desire, when ye pray, believe that ye receive them, and ye shall have them.

People, God can do anything. God will answer your prayers, but not as a result of your positive mental attitude. Other conditions must be met. 1. You must be a believer and believe in Jesus. 2. You must not hold a grudge against another person. 3. You must not pray with selfish motives. 4. Your request must be for the good of God's kingdom.[3]

Here's to keeping the main thing the main thing. To pray effectively, you need faith in God, not faith in the object of your request. If you focus only on your request, you will be left with nothing if your request is refused. Two words describe faith: sure and certain. These two qualities need a secure beginning and ending point.

---

3   See the following Bible texts for more information. **BELIEVE:** Matt. 21:22; Matt. 9:29; Mark 11:24–25. **GRUDGE/UNFORGIVENESS:** Ps. 66:18; Matt. 6:12; Mark 11:24–25; 1 Pet. 3:7. **MOTIVES:** John 15:7; John 16:24; James 4:3. **GOD'S KINGDOM:** John 14:13–14; Eph. 1:19; Eph. 3:20; 1 John 5:14.

The beginning point of faith is believing in God's character. He is who He says. The end point is believing in God's promises. He will do just what He says. When we believe that God will fulfill His promises even though we don't see those promises materializing yet, we demonstrate true faith. So, keep moving even in the rain. Just remember how He has brought you through and what He has brought you from. He is faithful to take you all the way.

While living in our home that no one but God gave to us, Tiff worked her job and I worked mine. The day came when my job told me I had to go, that I didn't fit in anymore. Well, yes, my feelings were hurt. I loved doing what I did as a wheelchair repair tech, but at the same time, I knew that God was still up to something. They wanted me to work on the Sabbath and I refused to in a loving way. They were going to take inventory that weekend and I informed them I was willing to come in on Sunday. So, who do I obey? God or man? Was I wrong for taking a stand for the One who feeds me, clothes me, takes care of me, who holds the worlds, the stars in His hands and little old me? If we are faithful to God, He will be faithful to us (1 Sam. 2:30).

Look what the Bible says. It asked me to never forget something no matter where I am or what I am doing. It says in Exodus 20:8–11:

> Remember the sabbath day, to keep it holy. Six days shalt thou labour, and do all thy work: but the seventh day is the sabbath of the LORD thy God: in it thou shalt not do any work, thou, nor thy son, nor thy daughter, thy manservant, nor thy maidservant, nor thy cattle, nor thy stranger that is within thy gates: for in six days the LORD made heaven and earth, the sea, and all that in them is, and rested the seventh day: wherefore the LORD blessed the sabbath day, and hallowed it.

All I was doing was obeying the Word of God, so I knew that all would be well because God's Word says that if we stand for Jesus, He will stand for us before His Father. Isaiah 41:10 says, "Fear thou not; for I am with thee: be not dismayed; for I am thy God: I will strengthen thee; yea, I will help thee; yea, I will uphold thee with the right hand of my righteousness." Now that's good news for what I was facing!

Four years with that company and now no job. I was cleaning out my van and getting ready to leave when a voice inside of me said to go back and tell them thank you for all they had done and that it was a blessing for me to have worked for and with them. They gave me a strange look when I reached for their hand to shake. I went home to tell my wife what happened and how my day went. What was God up to? I resolved to be strong in the Lord and I asked, "How much do I need to make a month to replace what I lost?" She told me. "How much do I need to make every two weeks?" She told me. "How much do I need to make a day?" Yes, you're right, she told me.

We used the logo that I made while in prison, the HIYH Bird. We named our business HIYH Medical Services and Repairs. Oh, and by the way, HIYH stands for How Is Your Heart. This name came from God. One day I was trying to understand how someone who knew the Bible from cover to cover could be so evil. Then I heard a voice say, "Don't worry about other people, David. How is your heart, is it for God or the world?" Business cards were made, and I started using the knowledge God gave me while in prison. A list was made of all the goals I had. Here is the list I wrote up while in prison and by God's grace all have come to pass:

1. Keep God first.
2. Register the name HIYH Ministries.
3. Become a non-profit.
4. Set up a website, e-mail, phone number, bank account, and PO Box for our ministry.
5. Purchase shirts and hats, calendars, tags for HIYH, business cards, and marketing items.
6. Patent the HIYH Bird Logo.
7. Get a tax ID.
8. Hire a manager for HIYH Ministries.
9. Learn piano and guitar.
10. Make CDs.
11. Write more songs.
12. Get my songs copyrighted.

13. Help people.
14. Spread the gospel of God's love.
15. Get to know the world.
16. Set up concerts.
17. Purchase vehicles.

I serve a Sovereign God. Wait a minute! What does the phrase "God is sovereign" really mean? Well, come with me to take a look at a Sovereign God. If you were to look up the word sovereign in the dictionary, you would find words and phrases like superior, greatest, supreme in power and authority, ruler, and also independent of all other in its definition.[4] To say it all is to say that God and God ONLY is in control! Can I show you what I've learned through my journey? Let us put on our spiritual glasses to see things closer. There is absolutely nothing that happens in the universe that is outside of God's influence and authority. As King of kings and Lord of lords, God has not limitations. God knows what you're going through, what you've been through and what you are about to go through. Let us look at just a few claims the Bible makes about God.

Revelation 21:6, "And he said unto me, It is done. I am Alpha and Omega, the beginning and the end. I will give unto him that is athirst of the fountain of the water of life freely."

Colossians 1:16, "For by him were all things created, that are in heaven, and that are in earth, visible and invisible, whether they be thrones, or dominions, or principalities, or powers: all things were created by him, and for him."

Romans 11:33, "O the depth of the riches both of the wisdom and knowledge of God! how unsearchable are his judgments, and his ways past finding out!"

Jeremiah 32:17, "Ah Lord GOD! behold, thou hast made the heaven and the earth by thy great power and stretched out arm, and there is nothing too hard for thee."

Psalm 103:19, "The LORD hath prepared his throne in the heavens; and his kingdom ruleth over all."

---

4   "Sovereign," Merriam-Webster, https://1ref.us/1g2 (accessed November 10, 2020).

Even Satan himself has to ask God's permission before he can act. Satan is the destroyer. Satan wants us to worship him and he ultimately wants to destroy us. But the Sovereign God, the God of love wants to love and save us. God alone is worthy of our worship. Just as peasants always bowed before their king for fear of offending the one who had the authority to take their life, God's sovereignty compels us to bow before Him. But unlike corrupt earthly kings who abuse their authority to terrorize their subjects, God rules in love. He loves you and wants the best for you and me.

> *But unlike corrupt earthly kings who abuse their authority to terrorize their subjects, God rules in love. He loves you and wants the best for you and me.*

Again, Romans 8:28 promises "that all things work together for good to them that love God, to them who are the called according to his purpose." He is speaking to you right now. I know you know it if you have made it this far in this book. And listen, that promise is amazing, not only because it demonstrates that an all-powerful God cares about you and me, but because it cannot be fulfilled unless the One who gives it is all-knowing, all-wise, all-powerful and all-loving. Just as the Ten Commandments are a testimony of God's character, this promise itself is a testimony to God's sovereignty when we come to know God as He is. You fall in love with Him because God is love. God is big, yet He cares about the smallest things. I want you to think about that promise in Romans 8:28 and the implications of that promise. Because God is sovereign and He loves you and me, then nothing, I repeat, nothing will ever come into your life that He does not either decree or allow. Consequently, no matter what you face or what faces you in life, you can take comfort in the fact that God is sovereign. So, How Is Your Heart?

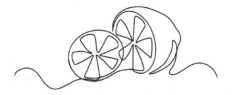

CHAPTER 30

All of us need an anchor. I told you way back in the book about a song called *The Anchor Holds*. That anchor is our faith in Jesus Christ. All of us need an anchor that will hold during the storms of life. What have you put your faith in? I write these things to give you hope.

Question: how important is it to have faith? Where do we find a faith strong enough to make it through the storms of life? The question is not if we have faith. Everyone has some kind of faith. The atheist has faith that his rational reasoning has removed the possibility of God. He has faith in his intellectual ability. Others have faith in their abilities, skills, connections, friends, family or themselves. Everyone has faith in something or someone. The question is what is your faith anchored in? Because, you bet as you are living and reading this now, sooner or later the storms of life will begin to blow. The question will become this: will the anchor of faith hold in what you believe in?

I have had cars, money and the things of this world and they have all vanished, *kaboom*, gone, bye-bye! In my growing, I have learned to trust God more and more. We are not given a good or bad life. We are given life. It is up to us to make it good or bad. You, I, we all have a choice how we use this life that we have been given.

As we started our business in the garage, God was our foundation as we built. We became a wheelchair wrecking yard. We took old chairs and parted them out. The parts that could be reused we sold at a discounted rate to those who could not afford much. We prayed and worked, worked and prayed and continued to repeat those steps. God was allowing doors to be opened and some closed, but we knew God was in all we were doing.

As our customer base grew, our garage became smaller and smaller. We knew the time had come to step out and step up and let God lead us to a business location outside of the house. How do you know when to move your business though? We prayed for God's guidance to go where He would have us go. I called my father-in-law Bob Lewis—that's a name we'll still use. He said we would know when the time came to move our business and as long as we treated it as a business, it would give back to us. And so, we built on those words.

Norman Peale says, "I place this day, my life, my loved ones, my work in the Lord's hands. There is no harm in the Lords hands, only good. Whatever happens, whatever results, if I am in the Lord's hands it is the Lord's will and it is good."[5] So, as the lemons kept being thrown at us, we kept making lemonade! Always in the back of our minds we asked, *what's next?*

We then moved the business from our house to a brick business strip of offices. We started out renting a 12' x 10' space for repairs and then another 12' x 10' space to keep chairs that needed repairing. We made it work with what God had given us. Our hope remained in the Lord that He was up to something great! As time went on, walls came down in that building. Another space became available next to our current spaces and thus we rented that too. That is when my wife Tiffany left the law firm and came on board full time as the OMG. What is an OMG you ask? It was my Office Manager Girl! Just a little name I gave her. Oh, how I needed her in that position full time and once again, God closed some doors and opened others so that she could be on board full time.

We only had one back door to these suites, and it was just big enough for a wheelchair to come through. We then added another suite for overflow until that suite started to overflow as well! Then we added one more suite for a total of four suites. This one was not connected, but it was used for overflow as well. Thus, it too overflowed and there was not any more space available at the time that would work for us. We made it work with those suites for a while though. One of our clients is the VA and for a period we were not receiving any jobs from them. I made a call to the VA

---

5   Norman Peale, "Quotable Quote," https://1ref.us/1g3 (accessed November 10, 2020).

to see what was going on. I was informed that we did not have a storefront and that was necessary in order to do work with them. I was also informed we did not have a garage to install vehicle lifts; therefore, it would not work. Well, I knew we did not have both of those things, I just did not know they wouldn't do business with us because of it. Now Hebrews 11:1 says, "Now faith is the substance of things hoped for, the evidence of things not seen."

Do you remember how you felt when you were very young (or maybe now!) and your birthday approached? Oh!! You were very excited and may have had great anticipation. You knew you would certainly receive gifts and other special treats, but some things would be a surprise. Birthdays combine assurance and anticipation, and so does faith! Faith is the conviction, based on experience, that God's new and fresh surprises will surely be ours. I knew that God had brought us this far and He would make a way. So, we started looking for a building with a storefront, a garage, parking and whatever else came with it. We went from our home garage to an office for $250 a month, to the other offices for a total of $700 a month. We looked and looked and looked. We eventually found a building that was 3,000 sq. ft. It came with two bathrooms, one kitchen, an all-glass storefront, garage, several offices and a conference room. More than we could ever have imagined! The rent was more than double our current rate at $1,500 a month. Could we make this happen?

We had been praying and trusting God to lead, believing that where He led, He would provide. After looking around at other places, we came back to this place. My wife and I both felt confident that this was the place God wanted us. We reached out to the landlord and the contract was signed.

> *We had been praying and trusting God to lead, believing that where He led, He would provide. After looking around at other places, we came back to this place. My wife and I both felt confident that this was the place God wanted us. We reached out to the landlord and the contract was signed.*

The previous tenants had left furniture, so we were blessed with some desks and things. God filled up the showroom, the conference room and even one of the rooms we turned into an aroma therapy relaxation room.

Since moving into our new location, our last daughter left home. We were in that five-bedroom house God had so abundantly blessed us with, but now with all the girls moved out, we believed God was moving us out too! It was a blessing to only be working about ten minutes from our shop; however, it seemed God was moving us towards the country. Thus, we began our search for property and a country home.

My wife Tiffany would search the Internet looking for property and houses. She found land in a little town called Farmersville. Farmersville! Here we go, oh no! I felt a little nervous about this move because we were moving a little distance from our business and our girls, but I was confident in God's leading. We had narrowed it down to two locations. We walked the first one and ended up finding a hungry stray dog. My wife just couldn't leave this dog here. I talked with a neighbor to see if the dog belonged to them. He informed me it had been dumped. They fed him from time to time, but he had no home. So, I told my wife, if he gets in the truck, we will take him. To our surprise, he got right in like he belonged! Due to the in-between of moving, we knew it wasn't time for us to take on a dog. We just happened to share this info with our pastor and his wife and they expressed interest in the dog. They had just decided they wanted to add to their family. So it was that Rex found his forever home! I share this little story to say that life isn't always about us. That is why we must have an open mind to what God's plans are because often our journey is about others. Let me tell you, Rex thrived, and our pastor and his beautiful wife were richly blessed, which in turn, blessed us!

Now let us back up a little. We found Rex at the first property, but we were not sure this was the one. We then went on to look at the second property. It was just under five acres. The electric, sewer and water were already in place which would be a huge blessing. As my wife exited the vehicle to walk the property these strong winds came out of nowhere. I looked at Tiffany and said, "This is the property, isn't it?" She smiled and said, "I believe so!" You see, my wife just had this connection with God and the wind. Many times in her life she felt God speaking to her with the wind. Let me just pause a minute and share with you one of her stories with the wind.

Tiffany was going through some hard times several years prior. Life just felt so heavy and she did not have the strength to keep fighting a certain something in her life. She could not see an end. She had sent her girls to church with her parents one Sabbath morning and she sat in her sunroom with all the windows open just weeping to God. She knew it was her choices that led her to the place she was at, but she begged God for something, anything to assure her He was there no matter what. She said no sooner had she stopped praying when she felt a gust of wind come across her. She looked up and out into her backyard. She lived in a neighborhood with huge, mature trees. She said that as this gust of wind came in through the windows and wrapped around her, the only trees blowing were the ones in her own backyard. NO OTHER trees were blowing. Now, tell me that is not God. That wind was just for her because that is how much the Creator of heaven and earth loved her. That is how much He loves us!

We believe in biblical hope, though it is an act. Hope acts on the conviction that God will complete the work that He has begun even when the appearances—especially when the appearances—oppose it. Remember this!

CHAPTER 31

We signed the contract for the land. Now we needed a house to put on the property. So, Tiffany was off again on the Internet looking for a home that we could fix up. There was a 1908 farmhouse on the Internet for sale. It was a few towns over, so we checked into how much it would cost to have it moved. We then went to look at the house. Oh, it was a fixer-upper for sure, but Tiffany could see beyond its current state and I trusted her. We made the offer. We got three bedrooms, one bathroom, one living room, one dining room, a kitchen and laundry room for $11,000 plus the cost to move it. Since it was just the two of us most of the time, this was a perfect house! We only had $7,000 of the $11,000 and the move was going to be $8,000. Not to mention we had to pay to have someone set up the electric, water and sewer. Hebrews 11:1 was repeated again, "Now faith is the substance of things hoped for, the evidence of things not seen." Oh boy, we took a step out. Romans 12:12, "Rejoicing in hope; patient in tribulation; continuing instant in prayer." The man who had the house took our $7,000 as a down payment and said we could move the house and pay out the rest later. This sounded great, but where was the rest of the money going to come from? Our God owns everything. He will not carry you where His grace doesn't cover you. We continued to walk in faith. We prayed and left it in God's hands.

Remember how I shared that my wife Tiff was no longer working at her job at the law firm? Let me tell you, she had paid into some disability during her time there. It was originally denied several times even though she had all the notes from the doctors. So, we just left that in God's hands. There was nothing more we could do about it. Little did we know at the time that God was just holding off on that money so that we would have it in just a time as this. She received enough to get the house moved and buy lunch for two! When God moves, God moves!

Romans 8:24–25, "For we are saved by hope: but hope that is seen is not hope: for what a man seeth, why doth he yet hope for? But if we hope for that we see not, then do we with patience wait for it."

You know, my friends—can I call you friends since you are getting to know me? Okay, I'll go on. It is natural for children to trust their parents, even though parents sometimes fail to keep their promises. Our heavenly Father, however, never makes promises He won't keep. Nevertheless, His plan may take more time than we expect. Rather than acting like impatient children … oh, how I had to learn! As we wait for God's will to unfold, we should place our confidence in God's goodness and wisdom, that somehow, someway, somewhere He will come through in His time. We are to act on our belief and keep being faithful.

We paid the mover and then it was time to MOVE THAT HOUSE! We closed the shop on the day our house was going to be moved. It was like a parade as we followed. *Wow*, I thought, *we are chasing our house*. Mailboxes were being pulled out of the ground in tight areas the house could not get through and placed back in the ground after the house was on the other side of them. There were flashing lights on the trucks. Cars were hitting the shoulder as we went by. What a day it was!

As we drove down our road to our property after about twenty-five miles, we heard a lady on her front porch say, "There's a house going down my road. No, a REAL house. I have never seen anything like it before." We arrived at our country home!

We told them where to place the house and then the work began. I started tree planting, grass and weed cutting, putting up a fence, putting down rock and so on. It was a job, but worth every minute we put into it. People ask us often, "How do the two of you work together, go to church together and … you're always together!" We say what God has put together, no man can take it apart and we chose not to allow that to happen. Matter of fact, a counselor told us that it would be the world against us, so we must remember we have God and each other. Isaiah 26:12 (NIV) says, "LORD, you establish peace for us; all that we have accomplished you have done for us." Only through Christ you can get things done. God, Tiff and I moved our entire household goods from the old house to the new one. We were able to get it done by God's grace.

We were moved in and driving back and forth to our shop. What used to be ten minutes was now forty-five to sixty minutes to work. And yes, we made that ride to and from work together for a while.

Chapter 32

Sometimes our business was up and down. God has many ways of getting our attention. One year, money was coming in pretty good. I was going to the bank and going to the bank if you know what I mean. If you don't, here it is. We were making a lot of money. Well, one day I said, and I think—no, I know—God heard me. My words were, "I'm tired of looking at money." Yes, that's what I said. I didn't tell my wife, but she noticed that business had slowed down a lot. One day she said to me, "Something is wrong, David. The phones just stopped ringing, customers aren't coming in, we aren't receiving new work orders. It's like everything has just stopped." I put my head down and said to her, "Well …" (and let me tell you it was a deep well that I was trying to climb out of), "I don't know if this has anything to do with anything, but I said out loud that I was tired of looking at money." When she looked up at me, that's when I realized I had spoken words into existence. We can speak life or death with our words so therefore, we must be careful what we say. Forgive us, Lord, we know not what we do.

My wife told me that I needed to have a talk with God and make things right. I did just that and the next week things started to change. We were not back to where we had been, but things were at least moving in that direction. Believe me when I tell you that I have never said that again! Nope, nope! Words can build you or break you. God was blessing and I was not grateful. Philippians 4:12 says, "I know both how to be abased, and I know how to abound: everywhere and in all things I am instructed both to be full and to be hungry, both to abound and to suffer need." Whether well fed or hungry I am content because I know God takes care of me. I was forgiven. And, oh yeah, I have learned to keep my mouth shut!

CHAPTER 33

The OMG, my wife Tiffany, was doing numbers on our cost of paying rent at $1,500 a month which came to $18,000 a year. She kept telling me about those numbers, but it was not clicking with me. She is very number-friendly which means she keeps us out of the red. What I did get was how much we had spent in rent for all the time we had been there. Three years and two months came to—ready for this? *$57,000.* That is American green dollars! Now I got it! It was clear! Remember the song *I Can See Clearly Now*? That is how I felt. Those numbers stood out. The Word of God says that when a man has found a good wife, he has found a good thing (Prov. 18:22). And how true!

Now it was time to do something again. Where do I go but to the Lord? I know God cares about how we spend our time and money. Paying all that money in rent and having nothing to show for it nor ever actually owning the space—it was time to move.

Okay, I have to take a break from writing. My wife and I are about to take a drive to Oklahoma. I will start back up tomorrow night. It is Friday sunset and I will rest until sunset tomorrow. Until then, my friends …

I'm back. As we looked to the Lord about putting up a building on our property, there was not any money to do it. We knew God was putting it on our hearts in order to save money, so we gave it to the Lord. If He wanted it, He would provide it. This we trusted. Because if God brings you to something, God will bring you through it! "The LORD is my shepherd; I shall not want" (Ps. 23:1). So, prayer was offered up.

"Lord, we are thankful for all You have done in our lives. All our blessings are from You. We used these blessings to help others.

Oh, God, You own everything, yet You share it with us. You said for us to be good stewards in all we do. We are trying to do that, Lord, show us the way that You want us to go. Your Word, oh God, says in Colossians 3:15–17:

> And let the peace of God rule in your hearts, to the which also ye are called in one body; and be ye thankful. Let the word of Christ dwell in you richly in all wisdom; teaching and admonishing one another in psalms and hymns and spiritual songs, singing with grace in your hearts to the Lord. And whatsoever ye do in word or deed, do all in the name of the Lord Jesus, giving thanks to God and the Father by him.

"Lord, we give our thanks."

Days passed. We know that God says yes, no or wait. God showed us to move forward. He put on our hearts to build a warehouse as we saved the money to do so. We saved to have gravel put down, concrete poured, framing put up, walls put in, rooms put in, wiring put throughout, a bathroom added, and water and sewage connected. We must be willing to be willing to be led by God, to stop and listen when He is speaking to us.

In Job 32:7–8 Elihu says, "I said, Days should speak, and multitude of years should teach wisdom. But there is a spirit in man: and the inspiration of the Almighty giveth them understanding." Understanding in what? Trust. Trusting God because He is—He is what? He is the God of gods and the Lord of lords. Trusting in who and what He is. It makes us stronger. He gives us knowledge; He gives us wisdom. He gives us love. He gives us strength. He gives us courage. He gives us peace. He gives us confidence. He gives us mercy. He gives us blessings. He gave us His only begotten Son! Jeremiah 17:7–8 says, "Blessed is the man that trusteth in the LORD, and whose hope the LORD is. For he shall be as a tree planted by the waters, and that spreadeth out her roots by the river, and shall not see when heat cometh, but her leaf shall be green; and shall not be careful in the year of drought, neither shall cease from yielding fruit." God can be trusted with anything, your hurts, your pains, your sorrows, your shame. Friends, I've been there!

Yes, the building was up! You think I said that I was tired of looking at money again? Nope, nope, nope! My God had come through many times for me and if you just stop and look around where He has brought you from to where you are now, you can see it too!

Psalm 34:8 says, "O taste and see that the LORD is good: blessed is the man that trusteth in him." We were up and running in our building that the Lord really owned. It was paid for and we had more people coming to us than when we had a storefront rental on a main street in the city. We wanted this building in the country because we worked with a lot of veterans (Army, Navy, Air Force and the Marines) and wanted them to be at peace while we worked on their equipment. We had overcome many obstacles in our life as I told you earlier. Our premarital counselor had advised us it would be the two of us against the world and we would need to keep God at the center to remain united. Oh, how true this has been!

> *If you are to reach your destiny in life, you cannot let the world own you. Rather, you must be all or nothing in your commitment to God. You must belong to Him and Him alone.*

We had family turn against us a few times along this journey. But if God is for you who can be against you? Question: does it really matter? God has said these things will happen as we live. And what does it matter if we live or die if we belong to the Lord? It is the truth. Be who He calls you to be. Isaiah 26:3–4, "Thou wilt keep him in perfect peace, whose mind is stayed on thee: because he trusteth in thee. Trust ye in the LORD for ever: for in the LORD JEHOVAH is everlasting strength." Build on Jesus and nothing else. We did overcome those family trials.

A prior boss, Travis Wortham from TYC, was there for us again to give us advice, encouragement and support. If you are to reach your destiny in life, you cannot let the world own you.

Rather, you must be all or nothing in your commitment to God. You must belong to Him and Him alone. God wants to transform our minds. Romans 12:2, "And be not conformed to this world: but be ye transformed by the renewing of your mind, that ye may prove what is that good, and acceptable, and perfect, will of God." Look and see for yourself. The battle is for our minds, the way we think. It's all spiritual!

God has good and perfect plans for His children. He wants us to be transformed people with renewed minds, living to honor and obey Him. He wants only what is best for us. He gave His Son to you and me to make our new lives possible! We—that is you and I—should joyfully give ourselves a living sacrifice for His service. You have heard that the mind is a terrible thing to waste. It is distressingly bad or serious. Our minds have been interrupted by Satan. With Jesus' help we need to resume after this interruption. In other words, when knocked down, get back up and keep moving.

We are called to not conform any longer to the pattern of this world with its behavior and customs that are usually selfish and often corrupting (Rom. 12:2). Many of us have wisely decided that much worldly behavior is off limits for us. Our refusal to conform to this world's values, however, must go even deeper than the level of behavior and customs we are used to. It must be firmly planted in our minds who God is and we must be transformed by the renewing of our minds. It is possible to avoid most worldly customs and still be proud, covetous, selfish, stubborn and arrogant. Only and only (do not miss this!) when the Holy Spirit renews, reeducates and redirects our minds are we truly transformed.

I have found out many things on my journey and one of them is that when God shows you who you are, He is giving you an opportunity to change. But He will not take our sinful nature away unless we ask Him to. It is up to us to keep it or let Him have it. That is love. Love does not force. For me, I am tired of letting things come between God and me.

Our business is still going and growing out in the country. We know who it did, we know who grew it. God gives us gifts so we can build up His church. To use them effectively, we must never forget this. We must discern that all gifts and abilities come from

God. Understand that not everyone has the same gifts. We must know who we are and what we do best. Dedicate our gifts to God's service, God's kingdom, and not to our personal success. Be willing to utilize our gifts wholeheartedly, not holding back anything from God's service. It is about God, not us.

Romans 12:9–11 says, "Let love be without dissimulation. Abhor that which is evil; cleave to that which is good. Be kindly affectioned one to another with brotherly love; in honour preferring one another; not slothful in business; fervent in spirit; serving the Lord."

People, God is the only One who can save us. Jesus is our intercessor and advocate. Remember that I said sometimes you go through the valley before God brings you to the mountain tops? I serve as the first elder at my church. The reason I share this is because I bring all my experiences with me about how good, loving, merciful, kind, and full of grace God is. The Bible says to let your testimonies be known to the world (Mark 5:19). And as you look at your life, you can see God's footprints where you have walked and where you are walking. He knows it all. Find out for yourself. But can I share something with you about the character of the God of Creation? Let us go mind renewing.

CHAPTER 34

I came across this in Psalm 77:13, "Thy way, O God, is in the sanctuary: who is so great a God as our God?" Who is so great a God as our God? What in the world is a sanctuary? So, I looked it up. A sanctuary is "a place of refuge or safety."[6] Hold on. Pump the breaks. Hold the phone. Tell that horse to stop! Oh, Lord, Thy way is in the sanctuary. So, I started to dig. There is something here along these pages in the Bible. What is it? Do I need to know it? Well, it's in the Bible, David, it is important to know. It does apply to you, David. The word important means this: "of great significance or value; likely to have a profound effect on success, survival, or well-being."[7]

Now this has my attention. I know that faith is not the ability to hold on to God—because sometimes I let go—but faith is the ability to believe that God is holding on to me. I'm slow on things, but once I get it, let me tell you, I come alive! But why is this in the Bible and no one hardly speaks about it? I saw the seventh-day Sabbath in there too and no one hardly speaks about that either. It sounds to me that God is trying to tell me something. I took a walk into the forest to see if I could find a path. My journey led me on another journey and this is what I found.

God loves us so much, but why are we not in heaven yet? Why has Jesus not returned as He promised? Could it be me? Could it be you? Could it be us? How can God take us to heaven without taking this sin infection with us? We are sinners continuing to sin. Remember that Jesus said in John 14:6, "I am the way, the truth, and the life: no man cometh unto the Father, but by me." I found out that He is doing something in this sanctuary that the Bible talks

6   "Sanctuary," Google, https://1ref.us/1g4 (accessed November 10, 2020).

7   "Important," Google, https://1ref.us/1g5 (accessed November 10, 2020).

about. Wowee! This is GREAT news indeed! For Jesus Christ can solve the sin problem, making eternal life possible for every sinner who will accept Christ's sacrifice and follow His way of separating our sins from us. Hello! There it is again. Right in front of me! Psalm 77:13 says, "Thy way, O God, is in the sanctuary: who is so great a God as our God?" Then I found out that God told Moses to build a sanctuary on earth like the one in heaven (Exod. 25:8). God gave Moses a look into heaven to see the heavenly sanctuary. Look at Hebrews 8:1–2 and you will notice that this verse is referring to the sanctuary in heaven. Come closer and look! "We have such an high priest, who is set on the right hand of the throne of the Majesty in the heavens; a minister of the sanctuary, and of the true tabernacle, which the Lord pitched, and not man" (Heb. 8:1–2). Then look at Hebrews 9:12 which says, "Neither by the blood of goats and calves, but by his own blood he entered in once into the holy place, having obtained eternal redemption for us." Remember I mentioned the renewing of minds? Well in Exodus 25:8 it says, "And let them make me a sanctuary; that I may dwell among them." If we let God dwell in our minds, He will renew our mind. I found this out also.

There were three parts to the earthly sanctuary! The outer court, the Holy Place and the Most Holy Place (Exod. 26:33; 27:9). According to the Bible, something happened in all three of these compartments. Exodus 31:18 says, "And he gave unto Moses, when he had made an end of communing with him upon mount Sinai, two tables of testimony, tables of stone, written with the finger of God." This made me take a seat right then to listen to the words that were being said. Everything found within the earthly sanctuary was made by man with the instructions from God— except the Ten Commandments. Those were written in stone. All ten. No one can change them. They were written by the immortal finger of God! These are things that make you say, hmmmmm!

Here are other things the Bible names within the sanctuary. An altar, a laver, the candlesticks, the table of shewbread, the altar of incense and the ark of the covenant where the law of God is.[8] Revelation 11:19 says, "And the temple of God was opened in

---

8   See the following Bible texts for more information. **ALTAR:** Exod. 27:1–8. **LAVER:** Exod. 30:17–21; Exod. 38:8. **CANDLESTICKS:** Exod. 25:23–30. **TABLE OF SHEWBREAD:** Exod. 25:23–30.

heaven, and there was seen in his temple the ark of his testament."
The Ten Commandments are there. After the cross, all eyes were
to focus on the heavenly sanctuary in which can be seen the law of
God. Why is this? God wants those of us who are living in these
days to know there is a right way and a wrong way to live.

We are told this: "Therefore by the deeds of the law there shall
no flesh be justified in his sight: for by the law is the knowledge of
sin" (Rom. 3:20). I will leave you with these Scriptures to see for
yourselves. But always pray before you read.

- Meaning of the gate in the sanctuary: Matthew 7:13–14
- Why do we put our hands on the offering: Leviticus 4:27–29
- Pillars—ten front, ten back, twenty on each side. Five pillars at the gate: Exodus 27:9–16, Exodus 26:37
- The name of Jesus: Isaiah 9:6
- God calls His place the altar. God says come to the altar: Matthew 5:23–24
- The Day of Atonement (At-one-ment): The whole chapter of Leviticus 16
- Altar in the court: Leviticus 4:6–7
- The color blue is to help us remember to obey: Numbers 15:37–40
- The color red is symbolic for the blood of Christ: Revelation 19:13
- The color purple is what you get when you mix blue and red, thus making us royalty to the throne of God. Purple can also represent wealth, prosperity and luxury: Judges 8:26; Ezekiel 27:7; Proverbs 31:22; Luke 16:19

Read and see what God reveals about Himself. I think there is
something to what David said—not me, but the other David. "Thy
way, O God, is in the sanctuary: who is so great a God as our

---

ALTAR OF INCENSE: Exod. 30:7–8. **ARK OF THE COVENANT:** Exod. 25:10–22.

God?" (Ps. 77:13). I have dealt with sins of many kind in this life of mine. When I stopped focusing on the sin and started to focus on the sin removal (Jesus' sacrifice), I started to see with no warning that through Christ, He was removing them as I was willing to let go, to repent. I can truly say that I know what it really means to let go and let God!

As Jesus is taking my sins that I confess, He pleads to His Father saying, "My blood has made him clean" (Heb. 9:22). You and I still have a chance for heaven as long as we have breath. This should give us hope. In Jesus we have hope. The universe is watching to see which side you and I will choose.

Look at Proverbs 7:1–3, "My son, keep my words, and lay up my commandments with thee. Keep my commandments, and live; and my law as the apple of thine eye. Bind them upon thy fingers, write them upon the table of thine heart."

- To be a good role model is:
- Knowing and obeying Jesus Christ
- Knowing and showing a good character
- Knowing and loving my children
- Knowing my abilities along with my gifts then repeat

I try not to judge people. I have a saying that if you listen to a person long enough, they will tell you who they are and what they are all about. God gives us knowledge to know right from wrong. The Bible says, the Lord gives, and the Lord takes away (Job 1:21). I believe the Lord gives life and takes away sin. If God gave a gift and took it back …. OH NO! My God is not an Indian giver. That is not His character.

As I learn to use my gifts more for God, He blesses me with more. We are moving forward now into Prison Ministry. We have been blessed with a 501(c)(3) Nonprofit, HIYH Ministries. We also purchased a school bus that we are turning into an RV, aka Skoolie, to use where God leads. Last but not least we have a van that we are donating to the Prison Ministry. We are active in our church and just going where God leads us. We have hope and it is our desire to help others know there is hope in Jesus Christ!

May you walk with Jesus always and have the hope in the Lord, the love, joy and peace that He can give you.

TEACH Services, Inc.
P U B L I S H I N G

We invite you to view the complete
selection of titles we publish at:
www.TEACHServices.com

We encourage you to write us
with your thoughts about this,
or any other book we publish at:
info@TEACHServices.com

TEACH Services' titles may be purchased in
bulk quantities for educational, fund-raising,
business, or promotional use.
bulksales@TEACHServices.com

Finally, if you are interested in seeing
your own book in print, please contact us at:
publishing@TEACHServices.com
We are happy to review your manuscript at no charge.